Deleuze and Guattari Studies
Volume 12 Number 4 2018

Infinite Eros: Deleuze, Guattari, and Feminist Couplings

Edited by Janae Sholtz and Cheri Lynne Carr

Edinburgh University Press

Subscription rates for 2019

Four issues per year, published in February, May, August and November

		Tier	UK	EUR	RoW	N. America
Institutions	Print& online	1	£166.00	£181.00	£190.00	$323.00
		2	£208.00	£223.00	£232.00	$394.00
		3	£259.00	£274.00	£283.00	$481.00
		4	£311.00	£326.00	£335.00	$570.00
		5	£352.00	£367.00	£376.00	$639.00
	Online	1	£140.00	£140.00	£140.00	$238.00
		2	£176.00	£176.00	£176.00	$299.00
		3	£219.00	£219.00	£219.00	$372.00
		4	£264.00	£264.00	£264.00	$449.00
		5	£299.00	£299.00	£299.00	$508.00
	Additional print volumes		£146.00	£161.00	£170.00	$289.00
	Single issues		£57.00	£61.00	£64.00	$109.00
Individuals	Print		£26.50	£42.00	£50.50	$86.00
	Online		£26.00	£26.00	£26.00	$44.00
	Print & online		£32.50	£48.00	£56.50	$96.00
	Back issues/single copies		£7.00	£12.00	£14.00	$24.00

How to order

Subscriptions can be accepted for complete volumes only. Print prices include packing and airmail for subscribers outside the UK. Volumes back to the year 2000 (where applicable) are included in online prices. Print back volumes will be charged at the current volume subscription rate.

All orders must be accompanied by the correct payment. You can pay by cheque in Pound Sterling or US Dollars, bank transfer, Direct Debit or Credit/Debit Card. The individual rate applies only when a subscription is paid for with a personal cheque, credit card or bank transfer.

To order using the online subscription form, please visit www.euppublishing.com/page/dlgs/subscribe

Alternatively you may place your order by telephone on +44 (0)131 650 4196, fax on +44 (0)131 662 3286 or email to journals@eup.ed.ac.uk using your Visa or Mastercard credit card.

Please make your cheque payable to Edinburgh University Press Ltd. Sterling cheques must be drawn on a UK bank account.

If you would like to pay by bank transfer or Direct Debit, contact us at journals@eup.ed.ac.uk and we will provide instructions.

Contents

This publication is available as a book (ISBN: 9781474439718) or as
a single issue or part of a subscription to *Deleuze Studies*, Volume 12
(ISSN: 1750-2241). Please visit www.euppublishing.com/dls for more
information.

with Kyle and Alex, always

Introduction: *Infinite Eros*

Janae Sholtz   Alvernia University

Cheri Lynne Carr   LaGuardia Community College, CUNY

This volume seeks to open spaces for the intermingling of feminist voices, prerogatives, and creativity with Deleuze and Guattari's work. The title *Infinite Eros* evokes the multiplicity of desire/s and Deleuze and Guattari's reformulated concept of love – a love that forestalls appropriation, unification or mastery while necessitating the opening of thought to the unfamiliar, the unknown, and the other-worldly. The idea of couplings, following upon Deleuze and Guattari's concept of becoming, implies a new capacity for intersubjective relation, one which seeks to find the particular, to undo identitarian prerogatives that limit our abilities to engage with one another, and to cause a mutual transformation that does justice to each.

I. Deleuzian Feminism: A History of Conceptual Couplings

There is a certain slippage in our use of the term 'coupling' to describe the relations between Deleuze, Guattari, and feminism. First, that couplings usually indicate a relation between two suggests, here, a necessary vacillation, a constant play and movement between three (at least): Where is the coupling? Which coupling? How coupling? Who's coupling? And, in light of Deleuze and Guattari's own reformulations of paradigmatic philosophical questions, we suggest that it is not a matter of deciding *between*, but of what couplings *can do*, allowing us to consider moving beyond the paradigm of two altogether – an intentional nod to Deleuze and Guattari's understanding of disjunctive synthesis that has been liberated from certain molar constraints (a 'both/and' rather than an 'either/or'). Moreover, this formulation speaks to the fact that even within the larger dyad of Deleuzo-Guattarian

Deleuze and Guattari Studies 12.4 (2018): 455–465
DOI: 10.3366/dlgs.2018.0323
© Edinburgh University Press
www.euppublishing.com/dlgs

Studies/Feminism, there is no singular path of analysis and there are a multiplicity of voices and conceptual personae within both Deleuze/Guattari and feminism(s) – an infinite relationality. This volume is an attempt to further these relations while acknowledging the cacophonies and harmonies of past couplings – to remain with these voices while simultaneously asking 'and . . . and?'

So many feminists have provided good reasons for feminist/Deleuze/Guattari couplings: the appeal has been attributed to Deleuze and Guattari as philosophers of difference, as critics of essentialism, representationalism, and foundationalism, as thoroughly committed to materiality, embodiment, and relationality, or as dedicated to a positive (non-phallogocentric) conception of desire and sexuality.[1] Yet, there have also been compelling arguments that Deleuze and Guattari scholarship is at odds with feminisms, perceptions grounded in a wariness about the appropriation of the feminine and/or disappearance of woman as a concern within philosophy, social/political concerns that the affirmation of dissolution is insensitive to the needs of differently situated subjects, as well as worries about Deleuze and Guattari's eurocentricism and thus their presumption to theorise the subaltern or minor at all, conceptual concerns that difference in-itself occludes the fundamentality of sexual and specific difference; and, finally, strategic concerns that becoming-imperceptible is insensitive to the exigencies of women fighting for political recognition.[2]

Over the last several decades, much of the work has been devoted to answering these critiques and attempting to either move beyond some of the problematic aspects or reappropriate these concepts within a more feminist purview.[3] Claims of the a-political and abstract nature of their work have been refuted; the import of their emphasis on locality and singularity has been re-evaluated; their complexification of dualistic models has been a powerful ally to feminist critiques of dualism; the implications of the rhizomatic, diagrammatic, and transversal nature of assemblages have been used to derive models of non-essentialising consistency which yields a minimal subject with the capacity for genuine relationality. In other words, many feminists have found nuance and potential in Deleuze and Guattari's project, and there is a rich counter-reading within feminist Deleuzo-Guattarian philosophy that, when taken together, illustrates the possibilities for alliance.[4] Even following the historical trajectory of its reception, we see transformation from initial wariness over the conceptual appropriation of woman vis-à-vis 'becoming woman' and 'the girl', to the incorporation of these concepts within the burgeoning field of 'girlhood studies' and new materialist feminist ontology.[5] However cautiously, feminists have interrogated how Deleuzo-Guattarian theories of desire, sexuality, and becoming provide an opportunity to reconceive sexual difference and move to more nuanced accounts of materiality, temporality, and embodiment.[6] More recently, Deleuzian feminists have taken note of how the multispecies-ism or species-egalitarianism and intra-actions of agential realism and emphasis on autopoietic assemblages indicative of new materialist feminisms (among others) resonate with or extend from Deleuzo-Guattarian emphasis on ontological immanence, material vitalism, and etho-ethnographical relationality[7] or have taken Deleuze and Guattari's concept of assemblage in productive directions for realigning and reconceiving feminist positions.[8]

II. Moving Beyond: The Beauty of the Razor's Edge

Beyond rehearsing the myriad feminist interpretations of becoming-woman (both the highly unsympathetic and the imaginatively optimistic) or extolling the progress from purely critical to more affirmative feminist analyses, we want to provide a space for new becomings and new voices in these interlocutions – while acknowledging that each of our author's contributions is marked by these zigzagging avenues of progress. Influenced by the stellar and groundbreaking work of feminist mothers, allies, and fellow feminist travellers, we hope to strike a new path of openness to exchange and creative interpretation that takes the idea of becoming, of productive encounter, at its most promising, transformative, and reciprocal word. Not to deny that these issues are important – they still remain touchstones to either be wary of or to be addressed, but what else is there – what happens if we bracket some of the conceptual issues to allow some unfettered encounters to bloom. To this end, we hope that our volume traces what one might call the razor's edge, echoing the intuitions of several feminists concerning the necessity for feminism of negotiating paradox,[9] and thinking, as it were, the macro and micro conditions of sexuality, femininity, thinking, and embodiment simultaneously (Gatens 2000).

We view the cover art in terms of this paradoxical edge of a Deleuzo-Guattarian feminist encounter – the need to acknowledge a feminist critique of the traditional encounter with the female form challenges us at the macro level, while at the micro level, we are implored to look with fresh eyes at the potentials opened up by reconfiguring our spaces of communication according to a Deleuzian immanent plane of desire and intensity. The work explores the surfaces between us or that conceive us, evoking 'indigenous cultures, [where] the painting on the skin was part of a gestation outbreak of different animal, vegetable and other becomings ... a "sacred" ritual of spiritual connection'.[10] Describing the collaboration between himself and Romina Ximena Maton as a 'living canvas', Deleuzian-inspired artist César Vallejos describes the process of becoming that exists between artist and model: 'there the painter is no longer an individuality and the model is not either, between them – in the middle and around it – a kind of "electromagnetism" of colours circulates'. As much as this painting illuminates a world of bodies and sexuality arises out of its immanent conditions – where the forces and affects of our human bodies intermingle with those of the cosmos – it also reminds us that to see beyond our particular predilections, our histories, and our wariness requires a kind of suspension, an ability to remain within the paradox of what we are seeing. César speaks openly about the 'edge' that must be negotiated and how his understanding of the living painting as a shared ritual is both a space of contention and release from patriarchal possessivity of the female form:

> For this painter it is not easy to fight against his own desires of annihilation, of possession that come from the macho and patriarchal shadows of power ... the small phallic-fascist soldiers that we men have in our daily register and of which we must take charge in order to recognise them and expel them.

César views his painterly process as an attempt to express non-possessive desire, a territory of seduction that fights against genital sexual possession to flow by populating the entire canvas with forces of colour and motion, transversal juxtapositions that meld figure and ground, living body and artistic gesture, so that the image 'can ascend through its shores, its slopes – towards a relation of sensations – in a plane of care and respect for otherness'. This artistic coupling speaks to the evocative possibility opened up by Deleuze and Guattari's stirring statement: 'one has painted the world on oneself, not oneself on the world' (1987: 220–1).

Foremost, we want to address the subject of love and desire through multiple voices and perspectives, not the least of which should be women's voices. In order to celebrate the heterogeneous space of love and desires, we have interspersed both original and existing poetic expressions on these themes among our essays. The reader will find contributions from Valentine Moulard-Leonard, Shinjung Nam, Katherine Moore, and Beat poet, Lenore Kandel. These women paint worlds of love and desire through their poetic expressions, adding to the multiplicity of voices that we are intent to uplift.

The issues of desire and sexuality also 'cut both ways' in relation to Deleuze and Guattari. While sexual difference and the acknowledgement of a specifically feminine sexuality has been essential to the promotion of female subjectivity and political recognition, the idea of productive and machinic desire that undergirds molar (social) constructs makes it increasingly necessary to think beyond the male/female binary: 'one can – and one should – strive to imagine different worlds where the essences, singularities and differences of life are not reduced to any single logic or set of relations' (Colebrook 2003: 8). Along with this reconceptualisation of desire as productive and connective, we can say that Deleuze and Guattari offer us a new conception of life – life as the singular relations that we are. Life is constituted, sustained, and amplified through connections and encounters, thus it is always constituted through difference, and these relations produce vital differences which are radically singular and happen at myriad levels of affective and intensive engagement with desire. Colebrook articulates the differentiations within life's connections both as a new understanding of sexual difference and as the motor of thought itself, suggesting that the necessary reconfiguration of sexual difference along an infinite number of paths and connections is one of the best opportunities for realising the feminist potential in Deleuze's philosophy. She suggests that feminism must see difference differently, in ways that further highlight the problem of the social and political meaning of difference, while giving credence to the infinite ways that life manifests difference, thought, and sexuality:

> If one *really thinks*, if one encounters what *is* in its radical singularity as possessing a power, force and potential – a capacity to relate – that goes beyond constituted terms, then sexual difference no longer explains the *thought (by a subject) of being*. Rather, thinking *is* sexual difference, the desiring response of life to life. (Colebrook 2003: 7; original emphasis)

Therefore, sexual difference is not between merely two, it is *between as such* – infinitely so – and indicates radical singularity and the need for attending to that which is beyond ourselves – the encounter, the coupling, and the becoming that ensues.

III. Infinite Eros

Just as Deleuze and Guattari understand their philosophical relationship as an act of love (Deleuze 1995: 7), which forestalls appropriation, unification, or mastery, this volume seeks to open spaces for the intermingling of feminist voices, prerogatives, and creativity with

Deleuze and Guattari's work and keep them open. As Hannah Stark so eloquently writes, 'philosophy is divorced from the prerogative of mastery and becomes an act of love. It is at those moments when the self is undone, and we are confounded with what is unknown ... that thought and creativity become possible' (2012: 105). *Infinite eros* speaks to philosophy as a dance of differences and the necessity of opening thought to the unfamiliar, the unknown, and the other-worldly. Interestingly, this is also how Deleuze and Guattari understand the emergence of a world – it is always through otherness, not *the* Other,[11] but a constant otherness that opens new potentials and vistas and that causes the proliferations of thought and of life that populate a world, and that push us beyond the concretisations of those worlds which may in fact inhibit us – political, socially, ethically, and creatively. It is the possibility of a revolutionary love:

> Knowing how to love does not mean remaining a man or a woman; it means extracting from one's sex the particles, the speeds and slownesses, the flows, the n sexes that constitute the girl of that sexuality. It is Age itself that is becoming child, just as Sexuality, any sexuality, is a becoming woman, in other words, a girl. (Deleuze and Guattari 1987: 277)

This quote at once represents an exhilarating ode to the potentiality of *eros* as a sweeping and infinite adventure *and* the problematic crux of Deleuze and Guattari's fraught relationship with feminism. As such, it is fitting. Love is never singular and linear, nor are relationships uncomplicated – at least the memorable ones. Feminism's response to Deleuze and Guattari is complicated, plural, transforming, and filled with zigzag lines of critique and convergence. Differences are both subtle and bold. The intensity of the *eros* springs from such paradoxes, such aberrant couplings, and it is this relationship to which we seek to do justice. It is with a keen eye to these difficulties and sensitive differences that our volume proceeds. Accordingly, our project stems from a wish to facilitate encounters between Deleuze and Guattari's work and the myriad perspectives of feminist theory which have come to enrich and transform the philosophical, political, ethical, and aesthetic landscapes. By titling this volume *Infinite Eros*, we evoke the multiplicity of desire and the reformulated concept of love that informs Deleuze and Guattari's understanding of relationality, endorsing the transformational potential of such encounters as an important gesture in creating new theoretical couplings between feminism and Deleuze and Guattari Studies.[12]

As Deleuze and Guattari say, 'We always make love with worlds' (1983: 294), but in order for this expression of love to happen, desire and love have to be liberated from their binary castings; rather than *eros* bound between a subject and its other, we are interested in the infinitude of affects and encounters that proliferate desire and institute becomings – of worlds, of new ways of being and thinking.[13] This model of becoming constitutes a new capacity for intersubjective relation, one which seeks to find the particular, to undo identitarian prerogatives that limit our abilities to engage with one another, and to cause a mutual transformation that does justice to each. This volume is an attempt to strike this delicate balance, to truly open a space for encountering new worlds while simultaneously advocating that we go beyond our own particular worlds, and it requires confrontation with some of our most cherished shibboleths, an exposure that requires vulnerability, humility, and strength. It is 'at those moments when the self is undone, and we are confounded with what is unknown (rather than what is known), that thought and creativity become possible' (Stark 2012: 106). What we have found is that feminism and Deleuze and Guattari's philosophy share a commitment to reinvention and infinite variation, to follow the paths of individual vicissitudes and the sufferings and joys of the worlds in which we live, and to courageously imagine better futures. Each contributor to this volume illuminates a new potential for aligning Deleuze and Guattari's philosophy with the desires and needs of a feminist future.

Which brings us to the idea of *infinite* eros. Deleuze says, 'the paradox of this pure becoming ... is the paradox of infinite identity' (1990: 2). If there is to be an ethics beyond recognition, such as requested by Deleuzian feminists such as Grosz (2002) or Stark (2017), it would be one that is based on love, a Deleuzian love that implies the infinite engagement with the otherness of our immanent and fluid relations to our selves, each other and the world – to become other through the myriad couplings to which we open ourselves – engendering new identities (ways of being, affects, modes of thought, desires) rather than recognising a singular Identity. It requires that we situate ourselves in the between of a paradox, to become who we are not and to open new worlds through these encounters as an infinite project. This project is not one of definitions, it is one of proliferations – of moving beyond critiques to encounters as an act of love.

Though *eros*, desire, and love set a tone for the kind of interactions in the volume, they are not the sole themes of consideration – rather, each contribution is an act of love through its variative expressions.

Each contribution represents a coupling encounter meant to transform rather than merely represent. We asked our contributors to think about what transpires in thinking between Deleuze and feminism, and each responded in their singular fashion, locating this overarching leitmotif within refrains of the political, the aesthetic, the technological, or the theoretical.

Notes

1. See Lorraine 1985 for common ground between the two; Olkowski 1999 for an account of Deleuze and Guattari's anti-traditionalism; Colebrook 2003 on difference; Braidotti 1994 and 2002 for commitment to relationality and political potential of nomadology; Grosz 1994 for a positive account of Deleuze's view of desire and material forces.
2. The critiques of Irigaray 1977, Jardine 1985, Butler 1987, Spivak 1988, and Braidotti 1994 set the early tone for feminist reception of Deleuze and Guattari's work. Kaplan 1996 reiterates and deepens some of the postcolonial concerns; Beckman's *Deleuze and Sex* (2011) registers both hesitation over repeating the Western tradition's tendency to treat subjects of desire and sex too abstractly and optimism in the potential of a productive rather than negative conception.
3. See Buchanan and Colebrook 2000 for the first compiled attempt to address this relationship.
4. Olkowski's (1999) analysis of feminist criticisms of Deleuze (Jardine, Irigaray, Butler, and Braidotti) is one of the paradigmatic and earliest examples of this nuanced counter-reading. She elaborates how Deleuze's theory of difference and critique of representation aid in the feminist project of undermining certain traditional philosophical/patriarchal paradigms. Goulimari 1999 also offers a critical reading of earlier feminist responses and a positive assessment of the minoritarian. Likewise, in her introduction to the special issue of *theory@buffalo8* on Deleuze and Feminism, Colebrook 2003 offers a succinct and informative analysis of the important ways that Deleuze and Guattari's philosophy was seen to be aligned with feminist prerogatives. Gilson 2011 addresses the four most persistent criticisms levied by feminists by interrogating singular concepts or problems within the larger context of their project. Most recently, Stark 2017 claims that Deleuze and Guattari's undermining of philosophical systems (that have oppressed women) offers feminism productive tools to shock feminism into finding new ways to address sexual difference, irrespective of whether their work is specifically focused on women's concerns.
5. On girlhood, see Coleman 2008; Renold and Ringrose 2008; Jackson 2010; Hickey-Moody and Rasmussen 2009; Rajiva 2014. Regarding new materialism, see Braidotti 2002; Dolphijn and van der Tuin 2012.
6. See Gatens 1996, 2000; Conley 2000; Grosz 2002; Pisters 2003; Burchill 2010; Braidotti 2003; Colebrook 2003.
7. Haraway 2016, 2003; Barad 2007; Bennett 2010; Thiele 2016; Sheldon 2016.
8. Currier 2003; Puar 2011; Ringrose and Coleman 2013; Ringrose and Renold 2014; Bogic 2017.
9. Citing Flieger 2000, Pisters claims that 'paradox is what we will have to come to terms with if we want to make a rhizomatic connection between feminism and Deleuze' (2003: 140).
10. Unpublished interview between César Vallejos and Janae Sholtz, April 2018.

11. See the appendix to *The Logic of Sense*, 'Michel Tournier and a World without Others', for Deleuze's elucidation of the operative role of the Other-structure in the creation of worlds (Deleuze 1990). See Stark 2012 for a feminist account of the importance of the Other-structure for a reconstituted account of love.

12. As Protevi writes, 'Love, is the call to enter [the] virtual and open up the actual, to install inclusive disjunctions so that the roads not taken are still accessible, so that we might experiment and produce new bodies' (2002: 184).

13. Stark argues that the Other-structure is a social rather than metaphysical *a priori* (2012: 104). It is a secondary manifestation which renders coherent differential relations. Whereas some have read his rejection of the Other-structure as pertaining to other people (radical solipsism), Stark sees it as a rejection of the *a priori* Other as a general category; by abandoning this structure, one can encounter the otherwise Other – a genuinely other expression of a possible world, suggesting that 'as a result of its continuous relations with others, the Deleuzian individual exists in a constantly unfinished state of individuation' (105) – which we relate to infinite *eros*.

References

Barad, Karen (2007) *Meeting the Universe Halfway: Quantum Physics and the Entanglement of Matter and Meaning*, Durham, NC: Duke University Press.

Beckman, Frida (ed.) (2011) *Deleuze and Sex*, Edinburgh: Edinburgh University Press.

Bennett, Jane (2010) *Vibrant Matter: A Political Ecology of Things*, Durham, NC: Duke University Press.

Bogic, Anna (2017) 'Theory in Perpetual Motion and Translation: Assemblage and Intersectionality in Feminist Studies', *Atlantis*, 38:1, pp. 138–49.

Braidotti, Rosi (1994) *Nomadic Subjects: Embodiment and Sexual Difference in Contemporary Feminist Theory*, New York: Columbia University Press.

Braidotti, Rosi (2002) *Metamorphoses: Towards a Materialist Theory of Becoming*, Oxford: Blackwell.

Braidotti, Rosi (2003) 'Becoming Woman: Or Sexual Difference Revisited', *Theory, Culture & Society*, 20:3, pp. 43–64.

Buchanan, Ian and Claire Colebrook (eds) (2000) *Deleuze and Feminist Theory*, Edinburgh: Edinburgh University Press.

Burchill, Louise (2010) 'Becoming-Woman: A Metamorphosis in the Present Relegating Repetition of Gendered Time to the Past', *Time & Society*, 19:1, pp. 81–97.

Butler, Judith (1987) *Subjects of Desire*, New York: Columbia University Press.

Colebrook, Claire (2003) 'Introduction', Barish Ali and Alla Ivanchikova (eds), *theory@buffalo 8: Deleuze and Feminism*, pp. 3–9.

Coleman, Rebecca (2008) 'The Becoming of Bodies: Girls, Media Effects and Body Image', *Feminist Media Studies*, 8:2, pp. 163–79.

Conley, Verena Andermatt (2000) 'Becoming Woman Now', in Ian Buchanan and Claire Colebrook (eds), *Deleuze and Feminist Theory*, Edinburgh: Edinburgh University Press, pp. 18–37.

Currier, Dianne (2003) 'Feminist Technological Futures: Deleuze and Body/Technology Assemblages', *Feminist Theory*, 4:3, pp. 321–38.

Deleuze, Gilles (1990) *The Logic of Sense*, trans. Mark Lester with Charles Stivale, ed. Constantin V. Boundas, New York: Columbia University Press.

Deleuze, Gilles (1995) *Negotiations, 1972–1990*, trans. Martin Joughin, New York: Columbia University Press.

Deleuze, Gilles and Félix Guattari (1983) *Anti-Oedipus: Capitalism and Schizophrenia*, trans. Robert Hurley, Mark Seem and Helen R. Lane, Minnesota: University of Minnesota Press.

Deleuze, Gilles and Félix Guattari (1987) *A Thousand Plateaus: Capitalism and Schizophrenia*, trans. Brian Massumi, Minneapolis: University of Minnesota Press.

Dolphijn, Rick and Iris van der Tuin (2012) *New Materialism: Interviews and Cartographies*, Ann Arbor: Open Humanities Press.

Flieger, Jerry Aline (2000) 'Be-coming-Woman: Deleuze, Schreber and Molecular Identification', in Ian Buchanan and Claire Colebrook (eds), *Deleuze and Feminist Theory*, Edinburgh: Edinburgh Press, pp. 38–63.

Gatens, Moira (1996) *Imaginary Bodies: Ethics, Power and Corporeality*, London: Routledge.

Gatens, Moira (2000) 'Feminism as "Password": Re-thinking the "Possible" with Spinoza and Deleuze', *Hypatia*, 15:2, pp. 59–75.

Gilson, Erinn Cunniff (2011) 'Responsive Becoming: Ethics Between Deleuze and Feminism', in Nathan Jun and Daniel W. Smith (eds), *Deleuze and Ethics*, Edinburgh: Edinburgh Press, pp. 63–88.

Goulimari, Pelagia (1999) 'A Minoritarian Feminism? Things to Do with Deleuze and Guattari', *Hypatia*, 14:2, pp. 97–120.

Grosz, Elizabeth (1994) *Volatile Bodies: Toward a Corporeal Feminism*, Bloomington: Indiana University Press.

Grosz, Elizabeth (2002) 'A Politics of Imperceptibility: A Response to 'anti-racism, multiculturalism, and the ethics of identification', *Philosophy and Social Criticism*, 28:4, pp. 463–72.

Haraway, Donna (2003) *The Companion Species Manifesto: Dogs, People, and Significant Otherness*, Chicago: Prickly Paradigm Press.

Haraway, Donna (2016) *Staying with the Trouble: Making Kin in the Chthulucene*, Durham, NC: Duke University Press.

Hickey-Moody, Anna and Mary Lou Rasmussen (2009) 'The Sexed Subject in-between Deleuze and Butler', in Chrysanthi Nigianni and Merl Storr (eds), *Deleuze and Queer Theory*, Edinburgh: Edinburgh University Press, pp. 37–53.

Irigaray, Luce (1977) *Ce Sexe qui n'en est pas un*, Paris: Minuit.

Jackson, A. Y. (2010) 'Deleuze and the Girl', *International Journal of Qualitative Studies in Education*, 23:5, pp. 579–87.

Jardine, Alice (1985) *Gynesis: Configurations of Woman and Modernity*, Ithaca, NY: Cornell University Press.

Kaplan, Caren (1996) *Questions of Travel: Postmodern Discourses of Displacement*, Durham, NC: Duke University Press.

Lorraine, Tamsin (1985) *Irigaray and Deleuze: Experiments in Visceral Philosophy*, Ithaca, NY: Cornell University Press.

Olkowski, Dorothea (1999) *Gilles Deleuze and the Ruin of Representation*, Ithaca, NY: Cornell University Press.

Pisters, Patricia (2003) 'Conceptual Personae and Aesthetic Figures of Becoming-Woman', *The Matrix of Visual Culture: Working with Deleuze in Film Theory*, Stanford, CA: Stanford University Press, pp. 106–40.

Protevi, John (2002) 'Love', in Paul Patton and John Protevi (eds), *Between Derrida and Deleuze*, London: Athlone Press, pp. 183–94.

Puar, Jasbir (2011) '"I would rather be a cyborg than a goddess": Intersectionality, Assemblage, and Affective Politics', *European Institute for Progressive Cultural Policies*, available at < http://eipcp.net/transversal/0811/puar/en > (accessed 11 July 2018).

Rajiva, Mythili (2014) 'Trauma and the Girl', in Marnina Gonick and Susanne Gannon (eds), *Becoming Girl: Collective Biography and the Production of Girlhood*, Toronto: Women's Press, pp. 137–58.

Renold, Emma and Jessica Ringrose (2008) 'Regulation and Rupture: Mapping Tween and Teenage Girls' Resistance to the Heterosexual Matrix', *Feminist Theory*, 9:3, pp. 313–38.

Ringrose, Jessica and Rebecca Coleman (2013) 'Looking and Desiring Machines: A Feminist Deleuzian Mapping of Bodies and Affects', in Rebecca Coleman and Jessica Ringrose (eds), *Deleuze and Research Methodologies*, Edinburgh: Edinburgh University Press, pp. 125–44.

Ringrose, Jessica and Emma Renold (2014) "'F**k Rape!'": Exploring Affective Intensities in a Feminist Research Assemblage', *Qualitative Inquiry*, 20:6, pp. 772–80.

Sheldon, Rebecca (2016) 'Matter and Meaning', *Rhizomes: Cultural Studies in Emerging Knowledge*, 30, n.p.

Spivak, Gayatri Chakravorty (1988) 'Can the subaltern speak?', in Cary Nelson and Lawrence Grossberg (eds), *Marxism and the Interpretation of Culture*, Chicago: University of Illinois Press, pp. 271–313.

Stark, Hannah (2012) 'Deleuze and Love', *Angelaki*, 17:1, pp. 99–113.

Stark, Hannah (2017) *Feminist Theory After Deleuze*, London: Bloomsbury Academic.

Thiele, Kathrin (2016) 'Of Immanence and Becoming: Deleuze and Guattari's Philosophy and/as Relational Ontology', *Deleuze Studies*, 10:1, pp. 117–34.

In her skin

Closing her eyes she knew exactly
Where she was
She was
Standing at the tips of her fingers
They found her breasts, her nipples, her sides, her thighs
And checked for the visible, a yesterday.

Still,
In time a darkness tides in,
Splash, into the
Touch of her fingertips upon her
Flesh,
Until the flesh of her touch, immense, from nowhere brings
Some stranger to this hour.

Flip of her hands
To keep her fingers free from
The darkness, this touch, this loss, this time
Won't see to it that the stranger departs for
The estranged is well finding home
Along the back of her hands
Behind her ears
By the gestures they hide
Where her tongue disappears
And one knee folds to kiss the back of another
There,
There, there, there, there she
Is
Lŏst
Loving

Original poem by Shinjung Nam, PhD Candidate, Department
of Anthropology, Princeton University.

Deleuze and Guattari Studies 12.4 (2018): 467
DOI: 10.3366/dlgs.2018.0324
© Shinjung Nam
www.euppublishing.com/dlgs

Love at the Limits: Between the Corporeal and the Incorporeal

Chantelle Gray   Institute for Gender Studies, University of South Africa

Abstract

New materialist frameworks have increasingly repudiated dualistic thinking and challenged representationalist views, which hold that discursive practices mediate our access to the material world (a core tenet of social constructivism). As it has become clear that the material cannot be considered inert, important questions concerning agency, politics and subjectivity have been raised. But while the significance of corporeality has been emphasised, Elizabeth Grosz, in an interview on her most recent book, *The Incorporeal* (2017), notes that: 'If materialism(s) cannot account for the immaterial events we experience and articulate, then it has a clear limit that it needs to address.' An important question this raises in terms of the mutual conditionings of love and one I will address is: How can we account for the immaterial space and time tracings of love without negating the material in the process? To answer this, I turn to Deleuze's *The Logic of Sense*.

Keywords: counter-actualisation, incorporeal double, love, quasi-causal, new materialism, Grosz

The humanities have seen a number of 'turns' over the past two decades. This is true of Deleuzian scholarship as well, which has tended in a number of directions, but in two markedly consequential ones, namely speculative realism (dominated by men, such as Ray Brassier, Graham Harman, Levi Bryant and Hamilton Grant) and new

Deleuze and Guattari Studies 12.4 (2018): 469–485
DOI: 10.3366/dlgs.2018.0325
© Edinburgh University Press
www.euppublishing.com/dlgs

materialism (dominated by women such as Rosi Braidotti, Jane Bennett, Karen Barad, Elizabeth Grosz and Donna Haraway). As a result, we have two streams of philosophy with a propensity towards dealing either with Deleuze's realism and the metaphysical or with his vital materialism The latter has been one of the more fruitful alliances between Deleuze and feminism, though this should be thought of in terms of a continuum, rather than a hard line.

At the heart of new materialism, and in the tradition of Deleuzo-Guattarian thought, we find that categories previously deemed binary are now held to be part of a complex co-imbricated ontology, as the work of Bennett, Barad, Grosz, Haraway, DeLanda and Protevi has shown. Studies such as these have given rise to more complex understandings of world phenomena, including gender and love. However, as Grosz notes in her recent book, *The Incorporeal*, it is 'the incorporeal conditions of corporeality, the excesses beyond and within corporeality that frame, orient and direct material things and processes ... so that they occupy space and time, [and] have possible meanings and directions that exceed their corporeality' (2017: 5). This, she argues, is not an anti-materialist project but, rather, one that explores the extra-material – the incorporeal conditions of the material. I would caution against the idea of 'conditions' here as the incorporeal (differen*t*iation) does not condition the corporeal (differen*c*iation) as such; that is, it is not a matter of extrinsic conditioning, but of immanent genesis. To put it differently, it is about the production of problems and the seeking out of solutions. Furthermore, this is not a problem of essences; it is not the question 'What is this?', which traps us in the aporetic and the transcendental (see Deleuze 2004: 94–5). This is a 'true problem', a problem of the virtual: 'the problem which orientates, conditions and engenders solutions, [which] do not resemble the conditions of the problem' (Deleuze 2001: 212). In other words, the solution does not subordinate the immanent processes of difference to the transcendent conditions of identity.

In this paper, I want to address the 'limits' of materiality and epistemology (without denying or diminishing the importance of these) by thinking about an ontology of love, which is at once incorporeal and corporeal. Accordingly, I want to think here about the mutual conditionings of love in terms of (1) the series schizoanalysis *and* feminism *and* love; and (2) the corporeal and the incorporeal, thus bridging the divide between new materialism and speculative realism by addressing what I see as the asymmetrical double direction or double dimension of incorporeality in *The Logic of Sense*.

I. The Limits of Love: *What is this?*

> Cynicism has said, or claimed to have said, everything there is to say about love: that it is a matter of a copulation of social and organic machines on a large scale (at bottom, love is in the organs; at bottom, love is a matter of economic determinations, money). But what is properly cynical is to claim a scandal where there is none to be found, and to pass for bold while lacking boldness. Better the delirium of common sense than its platitude. (Deleuze and Guattari 2004: 292)

This is as good a place to start as any when thinking about love: the delirium of common sense and platitudes. These are almost certainly banal, but they are not impotent; these are what drive and condition our conceptions and experiences of love, these are what make love profitable. 'This love', writes Enns, 'is a seductive deal, easy to market; we find in it all our best contemporary descriptions of ideal couple love' (2015: 33): #Love #Love is ... #Allyouneedislove. Even when we concede that love has, to a large extent, become the delirium of platitudes or common sense (the distribution of the sensible), we continue to be fascinated by love, by 'I love you', by the question 'What is love?' We have come to produce a whole history and imaginary of love in poetry, literature, music, other media and, also, in philosophy. Admittedly, the concept of love has received far more attention in the Analytic tradition, though a number of studies on love are currently being produced from a Continental perspective. Two volumes aimed explicitly at addressing love from this angle are the newly published books *The Materiality of Love: Essays on Affection and Cultural Practice* (Malinowska and Gratzke 2017) and *Thinking About Love* (Enns and Calcagno 2015).

Although the materiality of love is addressed in these volumes, we seem to continually find ourselves in the limits-of-love territory. Limits, for example, in terms of the concept and our conceptions of love born from socio-historical limitations and contingencies; the limit of contradiction (the dialectic), of patriarchy and humanist frameworks; limits, also, in terms of the *oeuvre* of Deleuze and Guattari because, as Stark argues, 'it persists throughout [their] work without ever being fully interrogated' (2008: 2). These limits are perhaps inevitable as addressing the concept of love in its entirety seems an inexhaustible task, yet it *does* deserve more attention in terms of Deleuze, and Deleuzo-Guattarian, philosophy for their 'unrelenting refusal to erase love' throughout their work (Stark 2008: 2). Having said that, a number of Deleuzian feminists have in fact addressed love in recent literature, as I will show in the subsequent section.

Nevertheless, there remains a 'limit' that I want to address in this paper with regard to the series feminism *and* schizoanalysis *and* love, namely that of the incorporeal. The reason that I want to address the incorporeal is that it has been primarily (though by no means exclusively) in terms of corporeality that feminists – especially new materialist feminists – have mobilised Deleuzo-Guattarian philosophy. As it has become clearer that the material cannot be considered inert, important questions concerning agency, politics and subjectivity have been raised. The importance of this intervention cannot be overemphasised as it disrupts a Cartesianism which has contributed significantly 'to a gendering of reason and rationality as masculine' (Stark 2017: 3), with the result that women have not only been excluded from the realm of thought but have also been divorced from the body. As Lloyd puts it: 'Rational knowledge has been construed as a transcending, transformation or control of natural forces; and the feminine has been associated with what rational knowledge transcends, dominates or simply leaves behind' (1984: 2). It is especially the female body and its association with supposedly 'feminine' aspects such as emotional love – as opposed to rational love – that has become 'left behind' or devalued. With this devaluation comes the 'imputation of wrongs and responsibilities, the bitter recrimination, the perpetual accusation, the *ressentiment*' (Deleuze 2006: 21) that we have come to know – have come to assume even – as constitutive of love. In addressing the 'I love you', Deleuze and Guattari argue:

> There is a presignifying 'I love you' of the collective type in which, as Miller says, a dance weds all the women of the tribe; there is a counter-signifying 'I love you' of the distributive and polemical type that has to do with war and relations of force (the 'I love you' of Penthesilea and Achilles); there is an 'I love you' that is addressed to a center of signifiance and uses interpretation to make a whole series of signifieds correspond to the signifying chain; and there is a postsignifying or passional 'I love you' that constitutes a proceeding beginning from a point of subjectification, then another, and yet another. (Deleuze and Guattari 1987: 147)

Is this all that is left of love, left to say about love? Is what we experience as love little more than the facialisation of love in the image of the despot – the foundation of subjectification, possession and power (*pouvoir*)? Has what we know and desire of love been subsumed by the bureaucratisation of love – a normative, proscriptive and prescriptive love-passion that necessitates a *connubial couple*: 'a *cogito* for two, a war *cogito*' (Deleuze and Guattari 1987: 128–9, 175, 131–3; 2004: 88–9)? If it has, then this is where we arrive at cynical love: the dogmatic image of thought.

Numerous fertile interventions have been offered, from both Deleuzian and non-Deleuzian feminists, such as Julia Kristeva, Hélène Cixous, Luce Irigaray, Kathy Acker, Dorothea Olkowski, Diane Enns, Isabelle Stengers, Claire Colebrook, Elizabeth Grosz, Patricia MacCormack, Hannah Stark and many others. Drawing on some of these theorists, I want to address concerns that do not focus solely or mainly on the epistemological underpinnings and materiality of love, but also on the immaterial/incorporeal aspects thereof, starting with concept of *becoming-woman*.

II. Sorcerous Love: Schizoanalysis *and* Feminism *and* Love

In *A Thousand Plateaus*, Deleuze and Guattari propose *becoming-woman* as one way of deterritorialising conventional, normative, and externally conditioned subjectivities. They argue not only that 'all becomings begin and pass through becoming-woman', but also that it is 'the key to all other becomings' (Deleuze and Guattari 1987: 277). They state, furthermore, that:

> On the near side, we encounter becomings-woman, becomings-child (becoming-woman, more than any other becoming, possesses a special introductory power; it is not so much that women are witches, but that sorcery proceeds by way of this becoming-woman). On the far side, we find becomings-elementary, -cellular, -molecular, and even becomings-imperceptible. Toward what void does the witch's broom lead? (Deleuze and Guattari 1987: 248)

A strange question indeed, for it may seem here that Deleuze and Guattari are advocating for womanly voids yet again: ways for women to be *the* void (Eris, the daughter of Void), to *be* void (the incorporeal Lilin-demon of shadows and dreams), to be *in* the void (Tehanu, Priestess of the Nameless Ones) – fading, falling, disappearing, gone, finally gone. *The becoming-woman that must become-imperceptible.*

Deleuze and Guattari's concepts of becoming-woman and becoming-imperceptible are, arguably, some of the main reasons why feminists have only 'recently and reluctantly' allied themselves positively with Deleuzian, and Deleuzo-Guattarian, philosophy (Conley 2000: 18). These by now well-known critiques of Deleuze (and Guattari) arise from the tension between the corporeal experiences of the female subject and Deleuze and Guattari's supposed preference of the 'extremely abstract subject' and the virtual (Stark 2012: 100). This is perhaps Jardine's (1985) main concern because, in explicitly stating that they are 'not interested in characteristics', but in 'modes of expansion, propagation, occupation, contagion, [and] peopling', Deleuze and Guattari seem to substantiate the claim that they value the incorporeal over the corporeal (Deleuze and Guattari 1987: 239).

The question these critiques are thus grappling with is: If the incorporeal is the asignifying, apersonal break, where is the corporeal subject of love? These are not invalid concerns, though they are based on a reductive and oddly essentialist reading of Deleuze and Guattari which denies their investment in the material – in material flows as either molar or molecular constituent parts of assemblages (Deleuze and Guattari 1987: 22–3, 39–74). Guattari writes, for example, that '[e]verything that pertains to the domain of rupture, surprise, and anguish, but also desire, the will to love and to create, somehow has to fit into the registers of dominant references' (Guattari and Rolnik 2007: 58). These dominant registers configure our relations, including our relations of love – to ourselves, to other humans, to all that is non-human – so that everything 'is gradually reduced to a mere form' (Guattari and Rolnik 2007: 118). These are very *material* considerations of love. But combating these material structurations of the figure of man and the figure of woman – in all their instantiations – requires a consideration of processes of differen*t*iation (the corporeal) as well as differen*c*iation (the incorporeal). This, as Rolnik notes, is 'precisely those processes that we could call, to quote Guattari, "becoming-woman"' (Guattari and Rolnik 2007: 112).

We return here to Deleuze and Guattari's understanding of sorcery, the pact, witches and witchcraft as 'a fearsome involution calling us toward unheard-of becomings' (Deleuze and Guattari 1987: 240). These unheard-of becomings, these sorcerous abominations, are the becoming-untamed/untameable of the female subject which, 'as opposed to the obedient vagina', MacCormack argues, 'will not be defined by production (family), chastity (church) or an acceptance of subjugation (state)' (2007: 820). Instead, the feminine subject becomes-witch, becomes-sorcerer, entering into a thousand uncanny pacts of becoming: the concurrent becoming-void of Eris, of the Lilin-demon and of Tehanu. At any rate, 'the void itself [is] the paradoxical element, the surface nonsense, or the always displaced aleatory point whence the event bursts forth as sense' (Deleuze 1990: 137). What we have here is, fundamentally, a problem of bordering: between the subjective and the asubjective, the corporeal and the incorporeal, the ascent to the surface and the renunciation of false depth; in short, a becoming-Alice, such that 'Alice is no longer able to make her way through to the depths. Instead, she releases her incorporeal double. It is by following the border, by skirting the surface, that one passes from bodies to the incorporeal' (Deleuze 1990: 10).

What might happen if we employ this becoming-Alice to think about the conceptions and actualisations of love beyond the binary territories of gendered sexualities which allow for narrow either/or categories: either male *or* female, heterosexual *or* homosexual, normal *or* queer, and so on? For Deleuze and Guattari, 'love observes no such boundaries, it is a mix-up, an intense, transgressive phenomenon, a "war machine" without bellicosity' (Flieger 2000: 43). Importantly, this is not a tallying function that allows merely for the description and experience of additional or otherwise kinds of gendered sexualities and experiences of love. For as significant as these are and have been in the recent past, they frequently remain within existing structures that formalise and reproduce them in specific ways. While the intensive phenomenon of the war machine does affect material actualisations, it is aimed primarily at perturbing the causal structures which give rise to embodied ideas and experiences of sexuality and love so that that the ordinary and singular points of structural arrangements are redistributed. Put differently, becoming-Alice is a witchy, sorcerous, demonic transgression aimed not merely at 'the exposure of male bias or interests within an otherwise good reason', but at the signalling of a climbing from the depths to the surface, following the border from corporeal bodies to the incorporeal (Stark 2017: 5).

If transposed to the tenor of love, we can thus say that love, as an incongruent combinatorial, is made possible by a disjunctive synthesis which both affirms the individual subject or body while, simultaneously, producing a cessation in or dissolution of the subject, replacing emotions and stable concepts with asubjective and asignifying coordinates on the body without organs. It is an affair of sorcery because it 'implies an initial relation of alliance with a demon' or the demonic, which, in turn, functions as the borderline between the subjective, corporeal experience of love and asubjective, incorporeal love which precedes all representation (Deleuze and Guattari 1987: 247). It is here, on the plane of immanence, where 'all concepts, ideas, thoughts, the Ideal, [and] the incorporeal' of love connect and become 'related to each other, to form points of convergence and divergence, to create alliances and tensions independent of the history of their formation or evaluation' (Grosz 2017: 136). Here, the sense of the void is complexified so that it no longer expresses only the virtual but also the asymmetrical relation between the virtual (differen*t*ial) and the extensive (differen*c*ial). This is important in thinking about an ontology of love as it relates to the problem of Alice releasing her incorporeal double, as I will clarify in the following section.

So far, we have seen some of the ways in which the series Deleuze *and* feminism *and* love has been mobilised, the ways in which this has provided us with schizoanalytic readings and mappings of love that, instead of moving in the direction of simpler constituents which very often end in binaries and homogeneity, provide us with an ever-increasing processual complexification towards 'ontological heterogeneity' (Guattari 1995: 61). This is a serial conception of love, of love in terms of the eternal return, of love as passage where we 'no longer have any secrets', having finally lost our faces, having become-imperceptible. Now we 'have become capable of loving, not with an abstract, universal love', but with a love that we 'shall choose, and that shall choose [us], blindly' (Deleuze and Guattari 1987: 199). We have begun to think also about the mutual conditionings of love in terms of individual and collective subjects, as well as the corporeal and the incorporeal, moving from cynical love to sorcerous love. Here we begin our passage away from the limits of love that allow for otherwise kinds of gendered sexualities and experiences of love. For while these, without a doubt, broaden our epistemological horizons, they remain all too often conditioned by the dogmatic image of thought; human-all-too-human. Here we ascend from the depths towards the surface, towards a sorcerous love: the single dicethrow that affirms all of chance so that whatever we will, we will 'in such a manner that [we] also will its eternal return' (Deleuze 2001: 7). Finally, then, we must address love at the limits, the incorporeal double of Alice, the double direction of the incorporeal. Paradox, after all, is that which destroys 'good sense as the only direction, but it is also that which destroys common sense as the assignation of fixed identities' (Deleuze 1990: 3).

III. Love at the Limits: The Incorporeal Double, the Double Direction of the Incorporeal

It is a strange prejudice which sets a higher value on depth than on breadth, and which accepts 'superficial' as meaning not 'of wide extent,' whereas 'deep,' on the other hand, signifies 'of great depth,' and not 'of small surface.'

> Yet it seems to me that a feeling such as love is better measured, if it can be measured at all, by the extent of its surface than by the degree of its depth. (Deleuze 1990: 336)

Having briefly addressed the series schizoanalysis *and* feminism *and* love, we now turn to the corporeal and the incorporeal where I attend to what I see as the asymmetrical double direction or double dimension of incorporeality as presented by Deleuze in *The Logic of Sense*. In *Difference and Repetition*, Deleuze initiates a critique against Kant's theory, which he contends accounts only for the synthesis of time in terms of the activity of a subject – this is why Deleuze will insist on the three *passive* syntheses of time. The main problem for Deleuze is that Kant's theory outlines only the conditions of *possible* experience, whereas Deleuze wants to think *real* experience in terms of an 'intrinsic genesis' (Deleuze 2001: 154). In other words, Deleuze is contending that the transcendental conditions of possible experience differ *in kind* from the immanent conditions of real experience, as the former inevitably subordinate difference to identity, resemblance, analogy and opposition. The conditions of real experience, on the other hand, relate to the simulacrum, 'the instance which includes a difference within itself' (69). To put it differently, the possible remains locked within the representation of concepts, while the virtual has bearing on Ideas. Whereas Kant argues that the transcendental unity of apperception is that which makes experience *possible*, Deleuze opines that what Kant is proposing is nothing more than the dogmatic image of thought, which cannot account for the genesis of real experience but merely explains how experience is conditioned and replicated (168–9). This, Deleuze argues, is the illegitimate tracing of the transcendental from the empirical:

> This play in the Idea is that of the differential: it runs throughout the Idea understood as multiplicity and constitutes the method of vice-diction (which Leibniz employed with such genius, even though he subordinated it to illegitimate conditions of convergence, thereby indicating the presence of a continuing pressure on the part of the requirements of representation). (Deleuze 2001: 279)

This is reiterated in *Anti-Oedipus*:

> But on condition that meaning be nothing other than use, that it become a firm principle only if we have at our disposal immanent criteria capable of determining the legitimate uses, as opposed to the illegitimate ones that relate use instead to a hypothetical meaning and re-establish a kind of transcendence. (Deleuze and Guattari 2004: 109)

In *The Logic of Sense*, the critique against Kant is taken up again, this time from a more structuralist approach. Here Deleuze argues that the Stoic fatalism found in Cicero's text provides us with 'the conceptual resources for affirming the disjunctive syntheses as such', insofar as it 'insists on the priority of pre-conceptual and non-corporeal compatibilities among events' (Bennett 2015: 26). Deleuze insists, however, that the relation between what he calls event-effects or surface-effects is not causal, but quasi-causal. As he puts it: 'Concerning the cause and the effect, events, *being always only effects*, are better able to form among themselves functions of quasi-causes or relations of quasi-causality which are always reversible' (Deleuze 1990: 8). He proceeds to use the example of an utterance by Bousquet, who exclaimed: 'My wound existed before me, I was born to embody it' (Deleuze 1990: 148). This statement may at first seem to indicate 'that the actual is sorted in two ways' (Bryant 2006). In other words, it seems to indicate a distinction between the actual, which 'corresponds to Chronos or the pure present which is not' – the embodiment of the wound – and 'the virtual which, in turn, corresponds to Aion or that which divides time into past and future' – the wound that comes before (Bryant 2006). Bryant goes on to argue, however, that he finds something missing from Deleuze's thesis when he claims that there is a substance akin to 'an ontological memory or pure past' that is 'detached from any subjects, [and] that inheres in all being' (2006). Instead, Bryant argues in favour of a more robust materialist position, which he sees as 'perpetually reproducing itself' materially and which 'discerns being composed entirely of actuality' (2006). But this 'detachment' does actually make sense in terms of Deleuze's thesis in *The Logic of Sense*, as I shall show.

The central problem in Bryant's argument is pointed out by Grosz, namely that new materialisms have a clear limit if they cannot account for the immaterial (the ideal), though the converse is equally true. As I see it, Deleuze's thesis proposes something different to what Bryant is arguing in terms of the two processes that constitute the logic of sense. The first is a logic of materialism, which includes the corporeal or extensive *as well as* the extra-corporeal or incorporeal – in the sense of incorporeal transformations – and which corresponds to Chronos or physical (circular) time. The second is a logic of idealism, or what Deleuze calls the virtual in *Difference and Repetition*, which refers to a pure or ideal incorporeality corresponding to Aion or virtual time and forms a straight line that is never present but always extending concurrently and *ad infinitum* into the past and the future. Thus, this detachment Bryant speaks of – this indifference that Deleuze calls sterile – 'cannot act or be acted upon' (Voss 2013: 18) as it differs in kind from the first logic of sense. Whereas the first logic of sense is that of the material and the effects of the material, namely incorporeal effects and affects, the second logic of sense is that of the pure ideational or incorporeal and is therefore detached from the material in a certain sense (see Deleuze 1990: 61–2). We are, in other words, dealing here with two ontologies that differ in kind. We find evidence of this in a number of places in *The Logic of Sense*, for example when Deleuze writes:

> The autonomy of the effect [that is, the autonomy of incorporeal transformations] is thus defined initially by its difference in nature from the cause [the pure incorporeal or the eternal return]; in the second place, it is defined by its relation to the quasi-cause. (Deleuze 1990: 95)

Hence, the incorporeal transformations do not change objects or subjects in a measurable or physical way – even though they are material processes – but in terms of their sense.

Two things become clear here. The first is that sense is produced and, we should be reminded, differs from signification (Deleuze 1990: 51, 71–2); the second is that incorporeality has a double dimension or simultaneous double direction: one that tends in the direction of surface-effects and one that tends in the direction of the ideal or virtual. This is the asymmetrical double direction of the incorporeal. Thus, sense comprises incorporeal surface-effects (or the conditions of possibility), as well as the ideal incorporeal (which is the genetic element of sense). What we have here is therefore a tension between Kant's transcendental philosophy or 'the transcendental conditions for something to have a sense' (Voss 2013: 6) and Deleuze's insistence that we have to account for a genetic power of sense. Deleuze's challenge is to present a new account of sense and the asymmetrical double direction of the incorporeal in such a way that this double-unknowable of the incorporeal – this paradox of sense – does not account for the possible or transcendental *and* immanent conditions of experience, but *only* for an immanent genesis. He does this by proposing that 'sense is not only the effect of the interaction of the corporeal', which includes socio-political and historical states of affairs, but adds that it 'also partakes in the structural organisation of an incorporeal surface that is attached to a quasi-causality' from which it differs in kind (Voss 2013: 21). This he will call the co-presence of a static genesis, which has the directionality of virtual to actual (Deleuze 1990: 141). He will then add a dynamic genesis to his thesis which has the directionality of actual to virtual and which must not implicate the static genesis (Deleuze 1990: 186). To this conceptualisation of genesis, we need to add another concept, namely that of counter-actualisation. Deleuze writes:

> But each time we must double this painful actualisation by a counter-actualisation which limits, moves, and transfigures it. We must accompany ourselves first, in order to survive, but then even when we die. [...] It is to give to the crack the chance of flying over its own incorporeal surface area, without stopping at the bursting within each body; it is, finally, to give us the chance to go farther than we would have believed possible. (Deleuze 1990: 161)

In thinking about love, we might deduce from this that love has a definitive corporeal existence in that subjects embody this incorporeal substance we call love and experience it physically, while also perceiving the incorporeal transformations it brings about. The danger here, however, lies in confusing the event solely with the actualisation process and its incorporeal transformations (that is, the material or corporeal). Counter-actualisation, on the other hand, is the affirmation of the eternal return, which is prepersonal and asignifying – pure incorporeality. The counter-actualisation is, effectively, that which enables the asymmetrical double direction of the incorporeal. In the language of *Difference and Repetition*, we might think of counter-actualisation as operating via the intensive, though it is closer to processes of redistributing singular and ordinary points in a virtual multiplicity; in other words, the recomposition of the plane of immanence. It becomes clearer now how we might think of the mutual, but asymmetrical, series of the corporeal and the incorporeal in terms of an ontology of love. But before we draw conclusions, I want to linger on the crack for a moment: the cracked identity of the stable subject which produces a redistribution of ordinary and singular points on the surface – hence, Alice's releasing of her incorporeal double. In short, we have returned to the critiques raised by Jardine. Thus, we *must* ask again: If the incorporeal is the asignifying, apersonal break, where is the subject of love – the subjective break? More importantly, where is the subjective break of the feminine subject?

The crack-up is often phrased by Deleuze as the question 'What happened?' *What happened to us, Dear, to our connubial love? What happened between yesterday and today? What happened that I no longer feel about this the way I used to?* We notice immediately that this is very different from the question of cynical love, namely 'What is this?' The importance of this change is that the question 'What is this?' or 'What is love?' is related to essences and, as such, 'prematurely judges the Idea as simplicity of the essence' (Deleuze 2004: 95). This is really a problem of consistency or Being, which goes back as far as Plato who proposed a theory of Forms or Ideas as a solution. These Forms or Ideas are abstract, eternal and changeless ontological properties, independent of ordinary entities or objects. They are often formulated as Beauty, Goodness and Truth – Love would also do – and can be said to be transcendent or metaphysical in nature. In contrast to this eternal world of Ideas, Plato postulates that there is also an intelligible world of transient relative forms, with the result that consistency is viewed as reliant on discontinuity. Whereas the relative form of love, for example, changes over time and even fades away (and is thus inconsistent and discontinuous), the ideal form of Love (which informs the relative form) remains consistent.

The problem of consistency – and also of metaphysics – is not a transcendent problem, but one which is immanent, emergent and contingent, as Deleuze argues throughout *Difference and Repetition* and *The Logic of Sense*. What this means is that, for Deleuze (and Guattari), consistency is derived not from discontinuity and inconsistency, but from continuity: the eternal return. When Alice climbs to the surface to discover that everything happens at the border, the crack-up has taken place and the depth of her body is deepened at the same time that the surface has widened. The crack-up, in the language of *A Thousand Plateaus*, is the disquieting molecular line that 'brings everything into play, but on a different scale and in different forms' (Deleuze and Guattari 1987: 199). It is the becoming-demonic of love: the concurrent becoming-pact and becoming-void of Eris, the Lilin-demon and Tehanu. It is becoming-Alice that *is* the phenomenon of bordering – the skirting of the surface where one passes from female body to becoming-woman to becoming-imperceptible. It is this transgression that perturbs both the corporeal and incorporeal causal structures that give rise to embodied ideas and experiences of sexuality and love.

What I am arguing is that the new materialisms – as a set of diverse, but overlapping, theories and practices – have, to some extent, reduced surfaces to depths in their focus on the agency and density of objects and bodies. This needs some qualification though – given that one of the major contributions made by new materialism to contemporary philosophy is the attention it pays to affect and sensation. Despite this, it seems to me that the focus remains mainly within the first logic of sense, namely that of materiality and incorporeal transformations, thus negating the second logic of sense, namely pure or ideal incorporeality. It goes without saying that this takes place to lesser and greater degrees, the latter found, for example, in the strong object-oriented ontologies. As a result, thinking about love in these terms only means that it remains largely trapped in cyclical time, treating the present in terms of *the* past and *the* future. The consequence of this is that even though there has been a strong and successful movement towards the dismantling of binarisms, this sense of the present does not move far enough in the direction of the border, remaining lodged in memory. Accordingly, what is needed is not only the overturning of Cartesianism, but also of Platonism. No longer *What is this?*, but simulacra in the Deleuzian understanding thereof, which is not concerned with essences or the extrinsic conditions of possible experience but with intrinsic genesis.

We can think of these two logics of sense in terms of Deleuze's argument that virtuals vary 'in kind as well as in their degree of proximity from the actual particles by which they are both emitted and absorbed' (Deleuze and Parnet 2002: 148). In terms of love, we may see this first logic as the *incorporeal materiality* that is so eloquently addressed by the new materialisms; that is, the ways in which bodies have the capacity to affect and be affected in their corporeal and sensory combinations. But to this series, another must be added which engenders a mutual resonance, namely the '*ideational material* or "stratum"' which has something 'unconditioned [in other words the sterile or detached], capable of assuring a real genesis' (Deleuze 1990: 19). This second series finds us, at last, on the straight line, the more terrible labyrinth: Aion.

Here, we are finally able to interrogate the double incorporeal of love. In the first series, this takes place in terms of the mutual conditionings of love as 'imbricated in a network of discourses about gender, sexuality, patriarchy, capitalism and the family' which, in turn, are embedded in 'ideological investments' which have shaped the ways in which we imagine, practise and theorise love and loving (Stark 2012: 99). In the second series of the mutual conditionings of love, we must conceive of the straight line capable of 'cutting into the thickness, of carving out surfaces', orienting and multiplying them (Deleuze 1990: 143) until the I cracks and the 'actual object becomes itself virtual' (Deleuze and Parnet 2002: 149). Here we move from female subject to becoming-woman to the imperceptible content of the eternal return, the ritornello, the incorporeal as the unconditioned or ideational which determines 'at once the condition and the conditioned' (Deleuze 1990: 122). Hence, the mutual conditionings of love are such that the series of conditions 'must be determined *along with*' the series they condition, and must, for that reason, 'change as the conditioned changes' (Smith 2012: 240), in mutual resonance, but all the while retaining something unconditioned, sterile and detached – the groundless ground. At this time, love can ascend from the false depths of the circle, the entrapment of the circle, the false eternal return of *ressentiment*, to the surface where the circle is replaced with a straight line. These are the two functions of the dicethrow which engender the processes of vice-diction; the first being that of 'intervening both in the determinations of the conditions of the problem and in the correlative genesis of cases of the solutions'; the second being the 'condensation of singularities' which, effectively, involves the redistribution of singular and ordinary points as the second function of the dicethrow (Deleuze 2001: 190). This redistribution of singular and ordinary points, in turn, allows for the production and experience of an entirely new ethics of love – one which does not negate the female subject as such, but which is intensified in its becoming-imperceptible, the true eternal return that returns only that which is affirmed. Not *amor*, not *amado* or *amadi*, not *amoroso*, but *amor fati*. I will end the discussion here by quoting Deleuze on Nietzsche:

> Not a probability distributed over several throws but all chance at once; not a final, desired, willed combination, but the fatal combination, fatal and loved, *amor fati*; not the return of a combination by the number of throws, but the repetition of a dicethrow by the nature of the fatally obtained number. (Deleuze 2006: 25–6)

IV. Conclusion

In allying feminist theory with Deleuzo-Guattarian philosophy, we find new ways of investigating the mutual conditionings of love not only in terms of human corporeal experience, but also in terms of the ways in which the corporeal and incorporeal are mutually conditioned. This gives rise to dynamic schizoanalytical frameworks and interrogations of the complex world phenomena we have to wade through on a daily basis. With the effects of capitalism, such as constant fatigue and anxiety, as well as the fast-paced technological societies we live in and the ever-increasing demands placed on us annually, monthly, and even daily, it is no surprise that we are sometimes reductionist in our theories. Perhaps we are all guilty of this to some extent. After all, we have to negotiate our ethics in more complex ways than ever before. What I have argued in this paper is for a movement towards complexity again; for feminist understandings that allow for all kinds of allies and alliances. I strongly believe that there are many more fruitful junctures to be explored between schizoanalysis *and* Deleuze *and* love, especially in bringing together epistemological and material understandings and experiences of love with an ontology of love that can account for both the logics of sense. I reiterate: not *amor*, not *amado* or *amadi*, not *amoroso*, but *amor fati*.

References

Bennett, Michael (2015) 'Cicero's De Fato in Deleuze's Logic of Sense', *Deleuze Studies*, 9:1, pp. 25–58.

Bryant, Levi (2006) 'Deleuze's Two Conceptions of the Virtual', *Larval Subjects*, 21 August, available at < http://larval-subjects.blogspot.co.za/2006/08/deleuzes-two-conceptions-of-virtual.html > (accessed 3 October 2017).

Conley, Verena Andermatt (2000) 'Becoming Woman Now', in Ian Buchanan and Claire Colebrook (eds), *Deleuze and Feminist Theory*, Edinburgh: Edinburgh University Press, pp. 18–37.

Deleuze, Gilles (1990) *The Logic of Sense*, trans. Mark Lester with Charles Stivale, ed. Constantin V. Boundas, New York: Columbia University Press.

Deleuze, Gilles (2001) *Difference and Repetition*, trans. Paul Patton, London: Continuum.

Deleuze, Gilles (2004) 'The Method of Dramatization', in *Desert Islands and Other Texts 1953–1974*, ed. David Lapoujade, trans. Michael Taormina, Los Angeles: Semiotext(e), pp. 94–116.

Deleuze, Gilles (2006) *Nietzsche and Philosophy*, trans. Hugh Tomlinson, London: Continuum.

Deleuze, Gilles and Félix Guattari (1987) *A Thousand Plateaus: Capitalism and Schizophrenia*, trans. Brian Massumi, Minneapolis: University of Minnesota Press.

Deleuze, Gilles and Félix Guattari (2004) *Anti-Oedipus: Capitalism and Schizophrenia*, trans. Robert Hurley, Mark Seem and Helen R. Lane, Minneapolis: University of Minnesota Press.

Deleuze, Gilles and Claire Parnet (2002) *Dialogues II*, trans. Hugh Tomlinson and Barbara Habberjam, London: Continuum.

Enns, Diane (2015) 'Love's Limit', in Diane Enns and Antonio Calcagno (eds), *Thinking About Love: Essays in Contemporary Continental Philosophy*, University Park, PA: Pennsylvania State University Press, pp. 31–45.

Enns, Diane and Antonio Calcagno (2015) *Thinking About Love: Essays in Contemporary Continental Philosophy*, University Park, PA: Pennsylvania State University Press.

Flieger, Jerry A. (2000) 'Becoming-Woman: Deleuze, Schreber and Molecular Identification', in Ian Buchanan and Claire Colebrook (eds), *Deleuze and Feminist Theory*, Edinburgh: Edinburgh University Press, pp. 38–63.

Grosz, Elizabeth (2017) *The Incorporeal: Ontology, Ethics and the Limits of Materialism*, New York: Columbia University Press.

Guattari, Félix (1995) *Chaosmosis: An Ethico-Aesthetic Paradigm*, trans. Paul Bains and Julian Pefanis, Bloomington: Indiana University Press.

Guattari, Félix and Suely Rolnik (2007) *Molecular Revolution in Brazil*, Los Angeles: Semiotext(e).

Jardine, Alice (1985) *Gynesis: Configurations of Woman and Modernity*, Ithaca, NY: Cornell University Press.

Lloyd, Genevieve (1984) *The Man of Reason: 'Male' and 'Female' in Western Philosophy*, London: Methuen.

MacCormack, Patricia (2007) 'Becomings-Cunt: Flesh, Fold and Infinity', in John Russell (ed.), *Frozen Tears III*, Birmingham: Article Press, pp. 800–38.

Malinowska, Anna and Michael Gratzke (2017) *The Materiality of Love: Essays on Affection and Cultural Practice*, London and New York: Routledge.

Smith, Daniel W. (2012) 'The Conditions of the New', in *Essays on Deleuze*, Edinburgh: Edinburgh University Press, pp. 235–55.

Stark, Hannah (2008) '"But we always make love with worlds": Deleuze (and Guattari) and Love', Online Proceedings of 'Sustaining Culture', Annual Conference of the Cultural Association of Australia (CSAA) UniSA, Adelaide, 6–8 December 2007, available at < http://w3.unisa.edu.au/cil/csaa/files/stark_edited_version.pdf > (accessed 22 August 2017).

Stark, Hannah (2012) 'Deleuze and Love', *Angelaki*, 171, pp. 99–113.

Stark, Hannah (2017) *Feminist Theory After Deleuze*, London: Bloomsbury Academic.

Voss, Daniela (2013) 'Rethinking of the Notion of Sense', *Deleuze Studies*, 7:1, pp. 1–25.

Kiki and the 'girl': A Moment of Reading between Deleuze and Feminism

Ritu Sen Chaudhuri   West Bengal State University

Abstract

The essay reads as a moment of alliance – a moment of reading of two disparate things together. The event of alliance remains inspired by Gilles Deleuze's theorisations of becoming. This marks the coming together of unrelated things – one into the fold of another – without being subordinated in the process. It reads an anime, *Kiki's Delivery Service* (Hayao Miyazaki, 1989), with Deleuze and Guattari's writings on 'the girl' (*A Thousand Plateaus*, 1987) – where the girl represented as 'real' in a fantasy meets the girl written as a metaphor in a theoretical intervention. This inflicts a sense of violence, of abstraction, to both the figures of 'girl'. On the one hand, Miyazaki's work, removed from the discourse of anime, is placed under a feminist scrutiny, while on the other hand, Deleuze and Guattari's notion of the 'girl', extracted from the logic of the original texts, is reinserted into feminist renditions. The two readings are coordinated by a specific intention. This is to imagine the feminist potential of the 'girl'. Occasionally the two works appear to talk to each other, yet sometimes they stand incommensurable. The texts animate each other without being subsumed by each other – inhabiting and following the movements to trace the other as fields of singularities which cannot be reduced to fixed identities or parallels. This transversal act of reading does not aim at coercing the Deleuzian notion of the girl upon Kiki, but rather looks forward to the conversations generated between the two narratives.

Keywords: girl, Kiki, becoming-woman, anime, Miyazaki, deterritorialisation

Deleuze and Guattari Studies 12.4 (2018): 486–504
DOI: 10.3366/dlgs.2018.0326
© Edinburgh University Press
www.euppublishing.com/dlgs

I. Introduction

Kiki is a thirteen-year-old country girl. She declares that she has to leave for her year-long witch's internship. She has to put up in a new town supporting herself. Her mother is taken aback. The surprise turns her magic potion black. It goes poof. She too is a witch. Her magic is affected by her feelings. 'You know, you tend to make impulsive decisions,' complains Kiki's black cat, Jiji. All the neighbours and her friends gather to see her off. Kiki mounts onto her broom. She concentrates. Her hair and dress flutter – producing a gush of wind. They fly south towards the sea. A sudden lightning crashes into rain! Kiki sinks into a sleeping train through the roof. She lands in hay and snuggles in for the night. Morning wakes her up. The train is moving. There waves the sea! A city is floating on it. Kiki and Jiji fly, over the sea – with the birds – past the clock tower. A tiny man from the clock tower catches a glimpse of this flight: 'My, a witch! how rare!' Kiki understands the town has not had a witch for quite some time.

Over an im-possible passage of becoming, beyond man–woman binarism, Deleuze and Guattari produce a girl. She becomes the 'metaphor' of becomings. She upholds a utopia – your ineluctable gender turns too many to be tied together. The utopic spark hovers around philosophical discourses without addressing the, symbolically and physically violated, reality of women across the world. Feminists cannot afford a dream – of post-gender, molecular interfaces – without attending to the gendered everyday. If they are transported to the utopic outside, who will fight out the still oppressive real/m? Yet, feminism cannot be reduced to the dominant logic of reason and reality. The real is repressive and reason is masculine. Feminists cannot live a reality without a dream of exceeding it! They cannot see a reality untainted by the unreal. Questioning incites anger. Feminist questions exceed the capacity limits of being replied. Debunking yields delirium. It cannot be contained in the phallocentric language. Revolution invites unreason. It bursts the boundaries, of reality and reason, asunder. Feminists cannot ignore Deleuze. I bring Kiki in the middle of a feminist delirium to interrupt the borders of real and illusory. She flies back and forth – her magic is drawn in reality. The anime helps, through the trope of flight, thinking over the mutual constitution of the molar and the molecular in the politics of feminism. The enchanted world of Kiki is replete with extra/ordinary instances of a girl's struggle for becoming what she is. To imagine that, I begin with a description of the Deleuzo-Guattarian theory on becoming-woman through the girl, interrupted by a few obdurate feminist questions.

II. Becoming Girl: Becoming Feminist

Deleuze and Guattari's thought of the girl is implicated in their concept of becoming-woman which is developed in *A Thousand Plateaus*. Being is always traversed by becoming. Becoming is always more than a simple transformation of a bodily realm of possible. It approaches the space and time beyond the androcentric. Becoming invokes an unconstrained past and a free future always also mediated by the present. This simultaneity of the past, present and future opens up to 'events'. The Event constitutes a surprise – a passage exceeding the molar structure of presence and subject/s. Surpassing the signs of recognition, becoming is always molecular.

For scholars like Alice Jardine (1985) or Jerry Aline Flieger (2000), neither the 'becoming-woman' nor the 'girl' is a project concerning female subjects. The notion of 'becoming', in its multiplicity and immanence, tends to efface the subject. The question is, what promise does the weight of this 'outside', pervading the realm of struggling women – destabilising their subjectivity – hold for feminism?

Deleuze's theorisation points to the political limitations of the molar structure, subsumed within the discourse of the dominant. The molar structure reduces feminist politics to androcentric terms. It repeats the structures, of aggression and insensitivity, which feminism opposes. One can read this mode of feminism as an act of inversion. Sometimes inversion, though a provisional move, is necessary. Deleuzian thought tries to push feminism, beyond the immediate level of social institutions, towards a greater politics. This is not a journey from immanence to transcendence, but rather the opposite. Becoming-woman escapes reduction to the 'molar' essentially characterised by the repressive connotations of the man–woman binary. This bears a positive potential for politics: 'If one is a woman, it remains necessary to become-woman as a way of putting into question the coagulations, rigidifications, and impositions required by patriarchal . . . relations' (Grosz 1994: 176).

Deleuze's *oeuvre* thinks the woman as the foundation of the whole process of becoming, acknowledging that, in the historical constitution of subjects, man is the primordial being and woman is what the man is not. Her subjectivity is splintered. Essentially marked as the other of man, always defined in opposition to man, she constitutes the epitome of otherness. Can this otherness be reduced to discursivity? Is the discourse, of the elemental otherness of woman, not mediated by her real oppressions? As Braidotti puts it, there are 'two questions: "How to free woman from the icon function to which phallogocentrism has confined her?" and "How to express a different, positive vision of female subjectivity?" [which are] inseparable' (1994: 115). The radical immanence of the subject through the decline of the phallogocentric premises of metaphysics and neutralisation of sexual difference damages the process of reclaiming a political subjectivity for women. Feminist contention is essentially sexed. Charged with a political consciousness of discriminations, feminism understands difference as a positive value, which functions in a net of interconnections. The feminist subject of knowledge, Braidotti adds, is 'rhizomatic (that is to say non-unitary, non-linear, web-like) ... endowed with multiple possibilities of inter-connectedness' (2002: 22). Braidotti conceives feminism as something which 'de-territorializes ... estranges us from the familiar, the intimate, the known' (2003: 13). It has the potential to explode dualities, such as the subject(ive)/object(ive) dyad, and push beyond conceptual oppositions. By retaining the category of woman, not being effaced either in linguistic determinations (pushing Butler beyond linguisticism) or in the courses of 'becoming' (pushing Deleuze and Guattari beyond radical immanence), Braidotti translates the Deleuzian call for multiplicity into feminist politics:

> Thus 'neo-materialism' emerges as a method, a conceptual frame and a political stand, which refuses the linguistic paradigm, stressing instead the concrete yet complex materiality of bodies immersed in social relations of power. (Braidotti, interviewed by Dolphijn and van der Tuin 2012: 21)

Yet, though Woman offers the very chance of becoming, Deleuze and Guattari do not pose the category as an exemplar of becoming-woman. They bring in the figure of 'girl' as the symbol of becoming. Being as always open to becoming is rather girl-like. The girl has a radical relation to the man. She is not just his other or opposite (woman) but the very becoming of man's other. '[B]ecoming-woman or the molecular woman is the girl herself' (Deleuze and Guattari 1987: 305). She holds the instability that surrounds being. The girl is beyond the sway of the rational and is invoked as the trope of becoming. This becoming does not reflect the lived experiences of a real girl. It does not take into account that 'as such female subjects do not have a privileged place in relation to the figure of the girl' (Stark 2017: 35). The category of girl, extending the logic of Freudian psychoanalysis, is reflected as the site of most aggressive privation and restructuring of bodies. The figure is decorporealised and transformed into an abstract universal moment. 'It is not the girl who becomes a woman; it is "becoming-woman" that produces the universal girl' (Deleuze and Guattari 2005: 277).

What is still significant is the way the figure has been deployed by Deleuze and Guattari. The girl is 'not defined by virginity; she is defined by a relation of movement and rest, speed and slowness ... She never ceases to roam upon a body without organs' (Deleuze and Guattari 2005: 276–7). She is a line of flight, constantly changing. The potential instability of the girl induces 'a multiplicity of micro-struggles, micro-particularities, operating not simply at the level of subject but also within and as subjects' (Grosz 1994: 176). Why is this relevant for feminism? As Pisters remarks, '[t]he BwO does not oppose the organs: it opposes the limits of the organism and makes multiple connections that go beyond the organism's organisation as it is traditionally defined' (2003: 110). Winning their battle against patriarchy is not the ultimate goal of feminists. This battle is being fought in molar terms, where women are 'endowed with organs and functions and assigned as molar subjects within a dichotomized economy of gender' (Burchill 2010: 88). To move beyond the majoritarian, feminism has to address the processes of becoming. It has to put into play the multiple micro-particularities and micro-femininities. The girl, with a body without organs, is the insignia of such micro-possibilities. The future of feminism, as Stark observes, 'subsists in the figure of becoming ... [where] the girl because of their nascent potentialities ... [undermines] the fixity of categories and the essentialism that has entrapped women in models from the past' (2017: 40).

Becoming involves a tortuous yet specific movement where becoming-woman marks an initial step towards becoming-imperceptible, an implicit sense of directionality identified by Grosz:

> Feminist struggles around the question of 'women's identities', 'women's rights', are thus only part of a stage setting for processes of becoming woman; and becoming woman is in turn the condition of human becomings, which in their turn must deterritorialize and become animal. (Grosz 1994: 179)

It is a movement towards 'being like everybody else' (Deleuze and Guattari 1987: 279), an absolute indissoluble anonymity. One would then no longer require being a woman to claim a radically other identity. Deleuze and Guattari create a radical anti-humanism that turns every element of the wider nature into modes of radical alterity. One has to remember that becoming woman or being imperceptible might not follow a definite sequence; it might not be amenable to our mundane calculations. It may always remain as an im-possibility within the molar itself, may appear as a moment of transgression, may permeate the mundane with a surprise.

III. Re/turning to Kiki: Questions of Subjectivation, Sexual Difference and Becoming-Witch

Following this line of argument, I read the intersection of the molar and molecular in the anime text *Kiki's Delivery Service*. Before I move on to think of the import of such interfaces, let me follow the argument of the text addressing a few basic queries. The anime stages the construction of Kiki's subjectivity through her effort to become a witch. The point here is that witchcraft, even if an 'unreal' work, needs real endeavours and relationships to be accomplished. Two related questions crop up. First, how can this process of subjectivation, charged with feminist potentials, be juxtaposed to a theory that obliterates the subject itself? Second, if there is no subject, who then is Kiki and what is she hoping to achieve? Let us address the first question first. This is through a conceptual structure called sexual difference. It helps understand how man/woman difference becomes congealed as a specific form of difference among beings. The problem lies in the conceptualisation of sexual difference as natural, not responsive to change. When this difference is recognised as a construct, the empiricism of the categories of man and woman becomes questionable.

This brings us to the second question. Let us reformulate it before addressing it. How would the abstract structure of sexual difference nuance the subjectivation of Kiki? One can posit the question of sexual difference in Deleuze's theorisation of the molar paradigm of subjectivity and the molecular space of becoming. The becoming initiated by the woman traverses boundaries – across other becomings – beyond binary oppositions. So, the man and the woman can be seen as events, within a field of singularities, pregnant with possibilities of unanticipated shifts from the prior structure of presence. The singular repeats and also interrupts the general (Deleuze 2004). The singular, in its repetition of the general, invokes shifts. Each repetition is different. Each repetition is marked by a difference-deferral, both temporal and spatial shifts. The singular is thus not fully derivable from the general – it remains undecidable. The structure of sexual difference helps understand the event of becoming-woman itself as a becoming. Becoming-woman is not a universal to be reflected in its particular enunciations. It is rather a generality enlivened in multiple moments of singularity. Every singular figuration, not inferable from the general, is new and thus undecidable. Embracing undecidability, feminism seeks to overturn the range of decisions which claim to chain it up to the molar. The anime girl Kiki is one such figuration. Kiki's subjectivity, implicated in singularity, bears some radical moments of possibilities. Her girlhood cannot be circumscribed into a molar episode of the coming of age drama. She has an ability to fly. She holds the impossible event of flight, the metaphor of outside, in her phenomenal being. She puts flying into practice! Living every day is not a mere relegation into the mundane molar. Her everyday remains animated by negotiations with the undecidable. This exactly is the feminist import of Kiki's subject formation. The specific style of Miyazaki's anime has some bearing on this.

IV. Anime Deterritorialised

Miyazaki's ingenious application of the medium of anime serves Kiki's simple yet stark diegesis most effectively. The anime portrays a fantastic world through at least three episodes of deterritorialisation – of forms, spaces and identities – each associated to the other. I begin with the genre of anime. In *Cinema 1* Deleuze explains:

> The screen, as the frame of frames, gives a common standard of measurement to things which do not have one – long shots of countryside and close-ups of the face, an astronomical system and a single drop of water – parts which do not have the same denominator of distance, relief or light. In all these senses the frame ensures a deterritorialisation of the image. (Deleuze 1986: 14–15)

Being the image of images, perhaps, animation stands doubly deterritorialised – where 'the drawing no longer constitutes a pose or a completed figure, but the description of a figure which is always in the process of being formed or dissolving through the movement of lines and points' (Deleuze 1986: 5).

Animation is literally bringing life or motion to the motionless. In anime reality has to be constructed (through scanning of hand-drawn images), from scratch, before it can be photographed. It does not as such evoke the, larger than life, sense of reality associated to live action film. The image in anime is far lesser than the real. As a style of animation originating in Japan (in association with manga), anime is starkly different from Western animations. As Thomas Lamarre (2009) observes, Miyazaki also differentiates his Studio Ghibli works from anime itself. He claims them as manga films. Unlike the Hollywood action film or anime based on cinematism (linked to technophilia), he opts for animetism (using minimal technology) which challenges 'a strict opposition between something like low tech and high tech, or between technique and technology' (Lamarre 2009: 43).[1] Thus, Miyazaki opens up an amazing interaction with technology.

Beyond the desperate attempts of modern technology to transform everything – curbing openness and indecision – Miyazaki includes nature and human beings into effectual resources. Lamarre notes how Miyazaki works:

> with sliding planes of the image in an attempt to produce a different relation to speed and technology. He favours the sliding sensation of speed … from the perspective of a bicycle or glider or flying broomstick … rather than zeroing in on a destination or target. (Lamarre 2009: 42)

Perhaps this brings Miyazaki's anime closer to a Deleuzian notion of cinema which 'is not just the unfolding of narrative, nor the presentation of desired objects for desiring viewers; cinema is a surface of intensities, effects of colour and movement, and an event that cannot be contained within a subject's point of view' (Colebrook 2002: 16). The anime provokes us, beyond the story of a girl, to linger in-between – spaces, colours, people and magic. 'At the level of narrative, too, Miyazaki avoids reaching a destination or … linear progressive movement and cyclical regressive movement. Even his stories tend to move laterally, sideways, diagonally' (Lamarre 2009: 42). Miyazaki's narratives are layered. The layers are not always top – bottom. They often go side by side. A story is interrupted by several other stories and tales, hints and references which are not necessarily sub-plots catering to the unfolding of the main storyline. Amidst the movement of the multiple other things the girl is seen to nuance her own journey. The focus of this essay is to see how the journey of the girl is always also implicated in these dispersed propensities.

The space inhabited by Kiki is deterritorialised too. It cannot be contained within cartography. The panoramic perspective, with marvellous colours, is at the same time meticulous and minute. The cities are located in a time-space in-between. Miyazaki draws a detailed setting of an incredibly simple, pre/post-capitalist, Mediterranean/Scandinavian, mid-twentieth-century city on the sea called Koriko. The name of the city is never mentioned in the film, except as a mark on a bus. Kiki's transistor, the cars, aircrafts and televisions seem to resemble mid-1960s models. Miyazaki wavers – between the pre-present-post-modern times – between the dreams-fears-fantasies of a girl. The subjectivity of Kiki, constructed within and beyond the narrative structure and the apparatus of the film, is also scattered. She is a village girl not like others of her age. She has magical powers. Kiki is a flying witch, yet not a fully qualified one. She is a trainee. She is not always good on her brooms. Unsure of her qualities, she remains confused.

'Kiki is one of the few Miyazaki films closely connected to the nitty-gritty of real life' (Napier 2001: 134). She seems to worry about how she is going to earn her living in a new town. Her services, as a flying witch, are being bought and sold (as she sets up a flying delivery service). This is not just an instance of 'defamiliarisation' – a technique Susan Napier brands Miyazaki's film with – showing that Kiki's 'fantastic powers are prosaically anchored in the need to survive in a modern money economy' (134). More than merely been rooted to the banal everyday, Kiki's magic is constituted by her relationships with others. There are multiple occasions in the film revealing that the surplus value of relationships, generated out of her surplus labour time (invested in the making of such relationships), cannot be reduced to the capitalistic norms of the money economy. Miyazaki produces a utopic economy which is mediated, though not subsumed, by money. This is also not an occasion, as Napier reads, of 'balancing fantasy with the real' so that the 'message of empowerment becomes far more effective' (134). Fantasy and real are often mutually constitutive. They are not too distinct to be amenable to the work of balancing. The call of feminism, as it is been read onto the diegesis of the film, resonates beyond the molar discourse of 'empowerment', whose aspirations towards equality (to men) rests on the logic of sameness. Feminist contentions cannot be reduced to an aim of acquiring a rightful place for woman within a paradigm set up along already-molarised options. Instead, the aim is to see how the 'place' itself remains in the fold of unforeseeable possibilities to out-pace the dominant.

V. Miyazaki and the *Shōjo*

Kiki has arrived at Koriko. She meets Osono the bakery woman. She begins a flying delivery service for Osono's bakery as her witch's internship. She makes a new friend, Ursula, a painter living alone in the woods. She also meets Tombo who takes her to ride on his bike. It has a big, pedal-driven propeller on it; when he finishes working on it, it is going to be a man-powered aeroplane. Riding the bike, they zoom down the hill. She lets herself loose and makes friends with him. They both, via different means though, love to fly. When Tombo wants Kiki to join his friends, including the snooty, well-dressed girls, who had always ridiculed Kiki's rustic looks, she gets mad and walks off. She falls onto her bed, exhausted, after the long uphill climb. She talks to Jiji. Jiji acts just like a cat. She tries her broom: she can't fly! Perhaps Kiki's confusing feelings about Tombo interrupt her magic.

Napier observes that Miyazaki has radically altered the role of *shōjo* (young girl, a subset of *shōnen* or minor):[2]

> Unlike the classic shojo, who is usually characterized by an ultrafemininity that is often passive or dreamy ... Miyazaki's girl characters are notably independent and active, courageously confronting the variety of obstacles before them in a manner that might well be described as stereotypically masculine. (Napier 2001: 124)

Shōjo, in Miyazaki's films, defy both cinematic and social norms. This defiance is not a simple inversion which could be described as stereotypically masculine. Through the surprises of becoming a girl, she travels ahead of stereotypes. Steering the story forth, yet not cannibalising it, she brings in different understandings of living every day. Miyazaki always introduces the *shōjo* as the central character. Challenging the cliché of Kawaii or cute girl (Kinsella 1995), Miyazaki ensures a nuanced representation of the girl. Through a nature–magic–culture conundrum his narratives tend to follow the journey of a girl. The occurrences in the course of her journey are not represented in the context of a man's reaction to them. She is not constituted by the gaze of the male protagonists of the film.[3] Instead, the brave and diligent *shōjo* frequently acts as a saviour of the people around her (Napier 2001; Iles 2005).

Unlike other popular trends of *shōjo* anime or *shōnen* anime (for young boys)[4] or pornographic anime (for adult viewers),[5] animes directed by Miyazaki (for children) do not produce an overtly sexualised image of the girl. She is often too young, or too absorbed in work, to be sexually active. She does not have a voluptuous body. Miyazaki's camera does not hang on her curves. The de-sexualised girl is no less stereotypical than a sexually active one. Sexual naivety defines an innately beautiful virgin as 'good' against the bad, sexually inquisitive, girl. The bad must be punished and the good should be owned. Sexuality of, both good and bad, girls must be controlled by men. Miyazaki does not await the 'innately beautiful' girl for a man. Her journey is sometimes mediated, even though not incorporated, by the possibilities of hetero-sexual couple formation. Her journey emphasises her worth, outlines her duty and demands her respect for the wider world of nature.

Miyazaki outlines the category of *shōjo* – as a girl on whom the force of gender standards has not yet been fully imposed. In *Spirited Away* (2001) we come to meet Chihiro – the *shōjo* who negotiates with a weird world of the spirits. She ultimately wins over her fears and saves her parents from a dark magic spell. Satsuki, in *My*

Neighbour Totoro (1988), befriends the wonderful wind God Totoro and through a magical journey learns to take care of herself and her sister Mei. In *Howl's Moving Castle* (2004) Sophie's appearance keeps shifting to that of an old lady. In her passage though the mystic spell Sophie turns resilient and lends support to Howl, the cursed wizard. In *Nausicaä of the Valley of the Wind* (1984), the warrior princess Nausicaä saves nature and the community after a toxic war has poisoned the whole environment. It is true that even in the face of this unconventional illustration of women, heteronormativity is thoroughly reinforced. While *Princess Mononoke* is one film ending up without such a hint, most of Miyazaki's other works clearly suggest heterosexual couple formation (Kiki and Tombo, Nausicaä and Asbel, Sophie and Howl). However, this is markedly different from dominant animations like Disney.[6] Miyazaki also links up girls with domestic chores. Sophie, Satsuki, Chihiro, Kiki are all found cleaning and cooking. Such activities liven up a positive and perhaps a liberatory air. Cleaning extends an aesthetic dimension to the living space. Food and cooking signifies a celebration of living every day. Domesticity does not circumscribe the accomplishments of the girl. Her deeds mark out significant spaces in the wider world–nonetheless, she honours the everyday activities and finds wonder in almost everything she encounters. The bonds of friendship and mentorship, connecting women of diverse ages, are uniquely projected in Miyazaki's animes. Beyond the insidious effects of internalised misogyny, women support each other. They do not blame, shame, doubt or underrate themselves and other women. This is something exceptional in cinematic standards. The Walt Disney animations recurrently establish the archetypally innocent and compassionate heroine as against a vindictive and often sexually unfulfilled older woman.[7]

The *shōjo*, although voicing her apprehensions about adult responsibilities, tends to defy the gender roles. Many of them hold the desire and/or ability to fly, a desire which they share with their male counterparts, though 'throughout Miyazaki's work, boys and girls have very different relations to flight' (Lamarre 2009: 78). Whereas boys have an affinity towards flying machines,[8] girls have a magical relationship with flight. Flight *per se* is both literally and figuratively linked to escape. When it is referred in the context of a girl, it attains a subversive connotation. The girl is forbidden from flying. She acquires the ability to fly as she undermines the prohibitive social. The 'line of flight' as a Deleuzo-Guattarian concept refers to a turn of escape, flowing into a deterritorialised/de-oedipalised possibility of becoming–not related to literal flying. Kiki finds her line of flight in the very act of flying. Magical power, to fly, helps her 'becoming everybody and everything' (Deleuze 1987: 279). Other animators like Walt Disney also working in the genre of fantasy apply the fantastic as a mode of sensational theatrical visual often unrelated to the subjectivity of the characters: 'Everything is on the surface, one-dimensional, and we are to delight in one-dimensional portrayal and thinking, for it is adorable, easy, and comforting in its simplicity' (Zipes 2006: 208). Disney uses fantasy 'only to transfix audiences and divert their potential utopian dreams and hope' (Zipes 2006: 333). Miyazaki's tales, on the other hand, come 'to question the degeneration of utopia' (Zipes 2006: 211).[9] He deploys magic to outdo the sway of capitalism and patriarchy. His magic is implicated in the journey of the girl and the development of her personhood. Flight opens up possibilities of breaking out of the repressive social. Is it the assumption that the girl, without the intervention of the unreal, remains incapable of subversion?

Miyazaki's *oeuvre* – invoking Japanese fairy tales, folk and Shinto beliefs (Baruma 2010), and respecting each ensouled element of nature – operates beyond the real–magical binary. Eluding one binary, does he adopt another inevitable one? He sees girls, stimulated by the energy of the spirit world, being closer to nature (Iles 2005). Miyazaki shares the eco-feminist and deep-ecologist 'principle of absolute respect for nature as the foundation of liberation from patriarchalism and industrialism. They see women as victims of the same patriarchal violence that is inflicted upon nature' (Castells 2004: 175). This logic falls into the trap of the asymmetric binary of nature and culture occupied in an inevitable masculinist bias. Miyazaki offers a more complex understanding of the nature – culture/technology relationship. 'Shojo appears to enable a displacement of technological boundaries, allowing for an exploration of the perimeters of boyish mechaphilia' (Lamarre 2009: 215). When it comes to the question of the girl, Miyazaki senses the mutual constitutiveness of nature and culture/technology. This generates an impression of technicity (Simondon 1980), a field of contingency exceeding, man/machine or living/non-living, binaries. It connects the geographic–ecological–economic–historical dimensions without being reduced to any one of them.[10]

Miyazaki's *oeuvre* signifies the girl or the *shōjo* as a figure of dislocation. More than just a passing stage in becoming a woman, *shōjo* signifies a performative space of displacements. She is still to be fully disciplined by the norms of gendering. She shifts the real–magic, nature–culture binaries and is drawn towards the Deleuzian girl, the signifier of becoming. However, the two girls remain far from becoming one. Does Kiki's living every day–in hardship and anxiety, joy and marvel–interrupt the becoming girl? The anime text addresses the sense of ambivalence through which the concerns of a growing-up individual like Kiki have to be articulated. Does this hold up her radical lines of flight? Does this, coercing a semblance of significance to her articulations, impede her deliriums?

VI. Kiki in the Delirious Drawing

'For Deleuze and Guattari the royal road to the unconscious ... is delirium' (Buchanan 2006: 119). The unconscious, unanticipatable as it remains, hints at the lack inherent in conscious knowing. The conscious intending self produces a secured identity representing the dominant, universal human. Moments of delirium, fracturing the monolithic subject, inaugurate possibilities beyond the androcentric exceeding sex–gender binaries. The unconscious is significant for feminism. The import of the unconscious, courtesy of Freud and Lacan, is incarcerated within the myth of Oedipus. Freudian psychoanalysis is grounded on the originary triangle–the child's incestuous desire for the mother, and the death of the father, ultimately repressed by the paternal interdiction. The speaking subject is instituted in its denial of the oedipal attachments–suppressing, silencing and phallicising the maternal realm. Deleuzo-Guattarian '[s]chizoanalysis, by contrast, begins with the partial objects or pre-personal differences from which the familial triangle is formed ... [and] opens the familial field out into the social, political and historical field' (Colebrook 2002: 133). Masculine and feminine identities are consequences of such multifarious alliances neither supporting nor foregoing the other. 'Schizoanalysis proposes to reach those regions of the orphan unconscious–indeed "beyond all law"–where the problem of Oedipus can no longer even be raised' (Deleuze and Guattari 2000: 81–2). The hints of the orphan realms of the unconscious are borne in delirium.

In *The Logic of Sense*, Deleuze reads Lewis Caroll's Alice, amidst her fantastic feats in the land of wonder, as a de-oedipalised metaphor of pure becoming. Pure becoming is an infinite identity of both directions and senses like past–future, plenitude–scarcity, activity–passivity, highness–lowness. This resonates with 'Deleuze and Guattari's description of the girl as a configuration of spatio-temporal relations–"a block of space-time"' (Burchill 2010: 88). Alice is a little girl yet to be reduced to a molar identity. She has a differential velocity, a line of flight, radically contrasting the weight of a maternal body. She traverses surfaces (shallow–deep), magnitudes (tiny–huge), scales (high–low), movements (extension–attenuation), perspective (sense–nonsense). Alice remains fractured into m/any. She, and her world, is delirious. Delirium cannot hold a proper name. Alice loses hers. 'The loss of proper name is the adventure which is repeated throughout all Alice's adventures ... when the names ... are carried away by the verbs of pure becoming ... all identity disappears from the self, the world, and the God' (Deleuze 1990: 3). The molar world with its God Oedipus, sliding into the language of events, disappears. Kiki passes through a world of fantasy. But unlike the 'conceptual persona/aesthetic figure' (Pisters 2003: 108) of Alice, she cannot afford to go 'inconsistent'. Kiki's adventures are wonderful, not strange. Her magic is inserted, as the structure of the narrative convinces her, within her every ordinary day. Kiki holds onto her proper name. The command of the proper, linked to property and propriation, tends to tie her to the rules of the society. The society–tangled in the patriarchal, fixed in terms of role–status–values–is always also open to change in the performative iterations (see Butler 1997). Thus, the molar comes upon the molecular. In her struggle to grow up, as an individual, Kiki runs into moments of delirium. Delirium here is not an ability-word to initiate the magic spell. It is an unanticipatable moment infusing the everyday.

While Kiki is bitterly suffering the loss of her magical powers Ursula invites her for an overnight stay. In Ursula's cabin, Kiki encounters a delirious drawing–a star-lit sky in the wood. There are huts and a chimney too–the sky is to fly–for the crows, for a lonely sheep, and the scorpions–for a horse who wings the face–of a girl and her tresses. Ursula draws herself over the rooftop waving her hands to the enchanted procession facing the moon. Who is this girl? Is she Kiki? Why is she looking different? She is not fully human–with an ear on her forehead, her hair overpassing the boundary of her face–where is her body? Has it been fragmented into her flight? Kiki looks different as she is being drawn in her 'becoming'.

Drawing, itself a line of flight, remains unanticipatable. It is not like tracing something which lies out there. Kiki is an excess and cannot be contained within the molar memory of how a girl should look. She is being drawn beyond the memory of the molar where the authority of man determines what is to be remembered and how is it to be commemorated. Flieger notes that exceeding the majoritarian memory,

Deleuze places woman within an 'unnamed anti-memorial' field. 'It would seem that "woman" is not even a noun in his lexicon'; she is 'the verbal gerund, designating "becoming" as a line of flight' (Flieger 2000: 47). Let me add two observations here. First, the noun 'woman' rooted in the Old English *wifmon* means the wife of a man. The palaeonymic engagements of a woman with her man cannot take her to surpass the binary mode. Second, the exteriority of 'becoming-woman' cannot be conceived in terms of the rule of language. We must recall that gerunds are verbals that function as nouns. Since gerunds are derived from verbs, they do express action. Also, because gerunds function as nouns, they occupy slots traditionally held by nouns in sentences such as subjects, direct objects and objects of prepositions. How can one save the woman from being reduced to a name? How can one see her in a work of becoming?

How does the drawing come into play here? Why does Kiki encounter the canvas which inscribes her in a flight? It is as if the molar is facing the molecular. Is 'facing' always also a work of providing a face? Yes and No. Yes, in the molar structure 'facing' involves interpellating one within the man–woman binary (privileging man as the standard). No, because the molecular is a movement beyond faces. Untying identification with the majoritarian face, becoming is a process of indiscernibility and defacement. Perhaps the drawing multiplies and outspreads Kiki's subjectivity – absorbed in her magical power to fly – as a haecceity. 'Multiplicities are defined by ... the line of flight or deterritorialisation according to which they change in nature and connect with other multiplicities' (Deleuze and Guattari 1987: 9). Paradoxically, the canvas draws her becoming through her face. Her body, bearing the marks of the binary, has been dispersed in her flight. Defacement here is the work of the literal face. Wiping out the majoritarian, it is only a face that remains. The drawing produces a moment of absurdity/delirium. The molar and the molecular look interchangeable. Kiki in her pure becoming, as she is being drawn, is in continuum with the real Kiki facing the canvas. Her desire to fly has produced the drawing (interrupting the unknowability of the act). The canvas has captured Kiki's desire to get absorbed in the multiplicity of nature. The oedipal law defines the psychic state of desire by the act of repression. Desire becomes desire as and when it is repressed. A girl is inhibited from doing things she wants to do. Flight appears to be the symbol of a girl's desire to be free – to get variegated into the multiple proclivities of nature and gender. Losing the weight of the mundane, permeating the drawing, she wings her desires.

VII. Conclusion

> Kiki stands enthralled. The painting has generated a sense of worth and splendour. She opens up elated. She talks about her loss, of magical power, and Ursula talks too.
> Ursula: All you can do when it gets like that is struggle ... I stop drawing. I walk, look at the scenery, take a nap. Or even nothing at all. Then all of a sudden, I want to draw.
> Kiki: Does that really happen?
> Ursula: It does ... Magic isn't just chants.
> Kiki: They say you fly by your gift.
> Ursula: Witch gifts. I like that. Witch's gifts, artist's gifts, and baker's gifts. Because of that, we have to go through some hardship.

Kiki, catching up to her witch's ability, grapples with settling down in Koriko – making people accept her for who she is. Her first letter home is a happy one. The resolution of her loss of magical power in terms of acquiring a place in the society and a heterosexual hint of couple-formation is a majoritarian move. This is not something to be abhorred. When a girl, in her own right, establishes herself within the molar, the act itself brings in some changes in the structure (that excludes her from such accomplishments). Let us also remember, the authority of the molar gets ruptured by performative shifts. Kiki puts her magical power into her everyday performativity. She regains her flight. Flight is what she desires and 'no society can tolerate a position of real desire without its structure of exploitation, servitude, and hierarchy being compromised' (Deleuze and Guattari 2000: 118). Kiki's narrative, although read as a depiction of a girl's subjectivity in its feminist implications, cannot be fully accommodated by the molar. I celebrate the fantastic world of Kiki's living every day mediated by molecular moments.

Enthused by Deleuze, feminists tend to move towards an unrestrained molecular field of desire emancipated from the oedipal constraints. The Deleuzo-Guattarian notion of the girl, soaring in the molecular, sketches such a moment of impossibility – 'beyond' the man–woman binary. The question remains, when do we get a glimpse of the molecular girl? Never, if we think of the molar – molecular in binary terms. 'It is thus necessary to conceive of a molecular women's politics that slips into molar confrontations and passes under or through them' (Deleuze and Guattari 1987: 276). Deleuze and Guattari fail to follow the nuances of these momentary mediations, of molecular in molar, as they are not interested in phenomenal woman caught up in her triumphs and achievements, oppression and agony. I do not reduce their engagements with 'the girl' to 'men's work' – calling upon her as a trope – resolving a philosophical crisis. I do not minimise the dynamics of Kiki's subjectivity into a staging of the negotiations between the molar and the molecular. I read two disparate texts together and look into the possibilities the girl holds for feminism. I think of some undecidable moments, of becoming, interposing the girl and the molar everyday. Kiki is a figuration of such a becoming – a movement towards the desire of opening up to the moments of singularity – unimpeded by the universal norms of subjectivity the majoritarian society impinges upon us.

Notes

1. Thomas Lamarre reads the works of Miyazaki through the Heideggerian questions concerning technology. He holds that '[i]n Miyazaki's animation, openness to the animetic interval translates into the need for a new god, and it turns out that only a girl can save us now' (2009: 85). I do not subscribe to his views on the futurity of the figure of the girl as the 'new god'. My politics is rather to emancipate the girl from the weight of the majoritarian that oppresses her on the one hand and turns her into a saviour on the other.

2. The history of the word *shōjo*, a cultural icon, is too complex to be well defined. In Japanese, girls do not refer themselves as *shōjo*. *Shōjo* is always addressed by a third party. Is this because they are not allowed to assert a separate space (signified by a name) for themselves? Does this, a style of speech, reveal the phallocentric implications of the semiotic structure? Perhaps yes. The women's movement or *ūmanribu* in the 1960s and 70s allowed *shōjo*, as a concept, to come to the foreground (Shigematsu 2012). It becomes possible to think of a separate category of the young girl further than the questions of getting married and bearing children. Gradually this space is invaded by commercial trends like Hello Kitty popularising the Kawaii (cute girl) image.

3. The notion of male gaze appears in Laura Mulvey's 1975 pioneering article, in which she develops a psychoanalytic theorisation of Hollywood scopophilia involving both voyeuristic and narcissistic visual pleasures. My allusion to Mulvey is not to claim a reading of Miyazaki in the line of feminist film theory. This is not also an unthought-of assertion that Miyazaki's films are beyond masculine gaze. The phallo-symbolic order is often too pervasive to be wished away. There is always a possibility of aporia and/or apparent slips. This is just to underscore that unlike other popular forms of anime or animation, Miyazaki's works are not overtly misogynistic.

4. The popular plots, including the sub-genres like magical girl (*mahōshōjo*) and boy's love (*shōnen-ai*), spin around the concerns of love (unreciprocated love, love triangles) and friendship shaped through the activities of high school life (Prough 2010).

5. Japanese pornographic animations often illustrate the female body in contradictory ways: 'frequently, the female body is indeed an object to be viewed, violated, and tortured, but other scenes show women's bodies as awesomely powerful, almost unstoppable forces of nature, although these two visions are hardly antithetical' (Napier 2001: 65).

6. Zipes 2006 argues that female characters in Disney films are essentially upheld by their male counterparts – fathers, boyfriends, supporting actors – perpetuating the male myth.
7. The plot of *The Little Mermaid*, released in the same year as *Kiki's Delivery Service* (1989), revolves around the conspiracies of the evil stepmother/sea-witch Ursula against the sixteen-year-old mermaid, Ariel. Whereas Ursula, the witch, conspires against Ariel, Ursula, the painter, opens up a whole new world of possibilities for Kiki.
8. Kiki's friend Tombo is labouring to turn his bicycle to an aviation apparatus. Tombo's adventure is not just a sub-plot of the anime. It holds autonomy to move alongside Kiki's journey.
9. Miyazaki holds an ambiguous relationship with the world of Disney. He is often referred to as the 'Japanese Walt Disney', yet his aesthetic and philosophical journey is radically different.
10. For a detailed discussion on technicity, see Sen Chaudhuri 2017.

References

Baruma, Ian (2010) *A Japanese Mirror*, London: Atlantic Books.
Braidotti, Rosi (1994) *Nomadic Subjects: Embodiment and Sexual Difference in Contemporary Feminist Theory*, New York: Columbia University Press.
Braidotti, Rosi (2002) *Metamorphoses: Towards a Materialist Theory of Becoming*, Cambridge: Polity Press.
Braidotti, Rosi (2003) 'Becoming Woman: Or Sexual Difference Revisited', *Theory, Culture & Society*, 20:3, pp. 43–64.
Buchanan, Ian (2006) 'Is a Schizoanalysis of Cinema Possible?', *Cinémas*, 16:2–3, pp. 116–45.
Burchill, Louise (2010) 'Becoming-Woman: A Metamorphosis in the Present Relegating Repetition of Gendered Time to the Past', *Time & Society*, 19:1, pp. 81–97.
Butler, Judith (1997) *The Psychic Life of Power: Theories in Subjection*, Stanford, CA: Stanford University Press.
Castells, Manuel (2004) *The Power of Identity*, Oxford: Blackwell.
Colebrook, Claire (2002) *Understanding Deleuze*, Crows Nest: Allen & Unwin.
Deleuze, Gilles (1986) *Cinema 1: The Movement Image*, trans. Hugh Tomlinson and Barbara Habberjam, Minneapolis: University of Minnesota Press.
Deleuze, Gilles (1990) *The Logic of Sense*, trans. Mark Lester with Charles Stivale, ed. Constantin V. Boundas, New York: Columbia University Press.
Deleuze, Gilles (2004) *Difference and Repetition*, trans. Paul Patton, New York: Colombia University Press.
Deleuze, Gilles and Félix Guattari (2000) *Anti-Oedipus: Capitalism and Schizophrenia*, trans. Robert Hurley, Mark Seem and Helen R. Lane, New York: Viking Press.
Deleuze, Gilles and Félix Guattari (2005) *A Thousand Plateaus: Capitalism and Schizophrenia*, trans. Brian Massumi, Minneapolis: University of Minnesota Press.
Dolphijn, Rick and Iris van der Tuin (2012) *New Materialism: Interviews and Cartographies*, Ann Arbor: Open Humanities Press.
Flieger, Jerry Aline (2000) 'Be-coming-Woman: Deleuze, Schreber and Molecular Identification', in Ian Buchanan and Claire Colebrook (eds), *Deleuze and Feminist Theory*, Edinburgh: Edinburgh Press, pp. 38–63.
Grosz, Elizabeth (1994) *Volatile Bodies: Towards a Corporeal Feminism*, Bloomington: Indiana University Press.

Howl's Moving Castle, film, directed by Hayao Miyazaki. Japan: Studio Ghibli, 2004.

Iles Timothy (2005) 'Female Voices, Male Words', *Electronic Journal of Contemporary Japanese Studies*, 31 January, available at < http://www.japanese-studies.org.uk/discussionpapers/2005/Iles.html > (accessed 1 December 2015).

Jardine, Alice (1985) *Gynesis: Configurations of Woman and Modernity*, Ithaca, NY: Cornell University Press.

Kiki's Delivery Service, film, directed by Hayao Miyazaki. Japan: Studio Ghibli, 1989.

Kinsella, Sharon (1995) 'Cuties in Japan', in Lise Skov and Brian Moeran (eds), *Women Media and Consumption in Japan*, Honolulu: Hawaii Press, pp. 220–54.

Lamarre, Thomas (2009) *The Anime Machine: A Media Theory of Animation*, Minneapolis: University of Minnesota Press.

Mulvey, Laura (1975) 'Visual Pleasure and Narrative Cinema', *Screen*, 16:3, pp. 6–18.

My Neighbour Totoro, film, directed by Hayao Miyazaki. Japan: Studio Ghibli, 1988.

Napier, Susan (2001) *Anime from Akira to Princess Mononoke: Experiencing Contemporary Japanese Animation*, New York: Palgrave.

Nausicaä of the Valley of the Wind, film, directed by Hayao Miyazaki. Japan: Studio Ghibli, 1984.

Pisters, Patricia (2003) 'Conceptual Personae and Aesthetic Figures of Becoming-Woman', in *The Matrix of Visual Culture: Working with Deleuze in Film Theory*, Stanford, CA: Stanford University Press, pp. 106–40.

Princess Mononoke, film, directed by Hayao Miyazaki. Japan: Studio Ghibli, 1997.

Prough, Jennifer (2010) 'Shōjo Manga in Japan and Abroad', in Toni Johnson-Woods (ed.), *An Anthology of Global and Cultural Perspectives*, New York: Continuum, pp. 93–106.

Sen Chaudhuri, Ritu (2017) 'Reading Ajantrik: Talking Technicity', in Debashree Dattaray, Epsita Halder and Sudip Bhattacharya (eds), *Following Forkhead Paths: Discussions on Narrative*, Kolkata: Setu Prakashani, pp. 251–60.

Shigematsu, Setsu (2012) *Scream from the Shadows: The Women's Liberation Movement in Japan*, Minneapolis: University of Minnesota Press.

Simondon, Gilbert (1980) *On the Mode of Existence of Technical Objects*, trans. Ninian Mellamphy, Minneapolis: Univocal Publishing.

Spirited Away, film, directed by Hayao Miyazaki. Japan: Studio Ghibli, 2001.

Stark, Hannah (2017) *Feminist Theory After Deleuze*, London: Bloomsbury Academic.

The Little Mermaid, film, directed by Ron Clements and Jon Musker. USA: Walt Disney Pictures, 1989.

Zipes, Jack (2006) 'Walt Disney's Civilizing Mission: From Revolution to Restoration', in Jack Zipes (ed.), *Fairy Tales and the Art of Subversion: The Classical Genre for Children and the Process of Civilization*, New York: Routledge, pp. 193–212.

Loud Ladies: Deterritorialising Femininity Through Becoming-Animal

Bethany Morris   Lindsey Wilson College

Abstract

Modern feminist movements run the risk of being appropriated by capitalist agenda and commodified for mass appeal, thus stripping them of their revolutionary potential. I would propose that in order for feminism to challenge this, movements may want to consider the subversion of subjectivity. Deleuze and Guattari's notions of becoming-animal and becoming-woman emphasise a subjectivity not confined by rigid identity, such as man/woman. However, feminists have challenged this theory, suggesting it is difficult to both fight for and dispel the very same notion, that is, woman. I argue that in first considering the feminine subject via the Lacanian understanding of 'Woman', it can be argued that feminine subjects can engage with becoming-animal to destabilise the notion of 'Woman'. Riot Grrls, FEMEN and Pussy Riot all demonstrate tactics which could be said to utilise becoming-animal and have had varying success in avoiding commodification.

Keywords: becoming-animal, Riot Grrls, FEMEN, Pussy Riot, commodification, subjectivity

Feminist activism has seen a renewal in popularity in contemporary American society. Issues range from sexual harassment to reproductive rights to representation in film and television. Writers such as Roxanne Gay and Ariel Levy are becoming more common names in popular literature.[1] Feminism has even become a fashion statement, with a surplus of merchandise available with slogans such as 'Smash the Patriarchy' and 'This is what a feminist looks like'. While addressing issues of sexual harassment, reproduction and representation is long

Deleuze and Guattari Studies 12.4 (2018): 505–521
DOI: 10.3366/dlgs.2018.0327
© Edinburgh University Press
www.euppublishing.com/dlgs

overdue, the rise in popularity of feminism as a brand and the ease with which it makes itself prevalent in contemporary American capitalist culture is something to be suspicious of. This, however, is not a new occurrence. The Riot Grrl movement, though it began as a fringe DIY movement, quickly became appropriated and sold back to young women and girls in the form of 'girl power', complete with rhinestone-encrusted camouflage and pink combat boots, illustrating how feminist movements become less able to challenge the status quo, and instead are become comfortable, falling into ideological traps of capitalism, disguised as individual freedom and empowerment and commodified for mass consumption. I propose that in order for feminism to regain its revolutionary and subversive potential, it must return to the feminine subject and subjectivity in general as the site of subversive potential. Deleuze and Guattari's (1987) notions of becoming-animal and becoming-woman are such ways to theorise this, which emphasise a subjectivity not confined by rigid identity, such as man/woman. However, feminists have challenged this theory, suggesting it is difficult to both fight for and dispel the very same notion, that is, woman. In first considering the feminine subject via the Lacanian understanding of woman, it can be argued that those in the position of woman seeking to loosen the rigidity of the molar woman may first engage with becoming-animal to destabilise the notion of woman while also engaging in feminist activism. To do this, I use the Riot Grrl movement, which allows me to track its progress and demonstrate what it was able to accomplish as a body unto itself before it became captured and commodified, as well as the contemporary groups, Pussy Riot and FEMEN, which seem to be employing different tactics than some American branches of feminism.

In order to do this, a theory of how the Lacanian feminine subject is conceptualised and related to Deleuze and Guattari's becoming-woman is required. For both psychoanalysis and schizoanalysis, it is crucial to understand that there is no essential feminine, but rather contexts in which certain bodies and ways of being are demarcated as feminine, and that demarcation corresponds to a failure of signification. According to Lacan, young boys are socialised to misrecognise themselves as possessing the phallus, the signifier of the Other's desire, and are therefore completely cut from the Other, what he refers to as castration (1975). The benefit of this lack is that they are able to circulate signifiers which correspond to their experience of reality. The Symbolic, the level in which language constructs us, holds more authority. However, for women, Lacan argues, signifiers can never adequately represent them because the very existence of a signifier is phallic. Therefore, women are only partially castrated, and are left with a foot in language, and a foot outside of language that can be understood as undifferentiated surplus. As Lacan also suggests, this failure of the signifier allows for those on the designated feminine side to engage in a sort of masquerade, in which there is a game of sorts in which the woman pretends to correspond to the signifier that represents her (2007). The notion of 'woman' and the eternal question 'What does a woman want?' are taken up and articulated depending on the signifiers available at a particular contextual moment. However, in a post-anthropocentric move, Deleuze and Guattari suggest that this status of Woman is what allows her access to different modes of becoming which similarly elude signification. They argue that becoming woman is the first step for all becomings as it is the first move away from Oedipalised Subjectivation.

Becoming-woman, however, is not without its criticisms. Braidotti (2003) suggests that in positing becoming-woman as the means for all becomings to move towards a multiplicity, while simultaneously calling for its dismissal, attempts to bypass phallocentric representation on the promise of something new, without properly contending with sexual difference as a metaphysical and epistemological difference. She notes that Deleuze, though sympathetic to feminist projects which need to reclaim some sort of female identity, also suggests that 'it is dangerous to confine oneself to such a subject, which does not function without drying up a spring or stopping a flow' (Deleuze and Guattari 1987: 276). Braidotti contends with this contradiction through a return to the body and affect as the site to develop an approach she refers to as nomadic subjectivity. Nomadic subjectivity is premised on utilising identity monikers when the need calls for it, specifically when one finds oneself in hostile territory, which allows the subject to rely on those significations that designate her as a being. However, the trick for Braidotti is to apprehend the moment when those signifiers must be exchanged for new ones, a difficult trick as neoliberal identity politics become more and more pervasive. While Braidotti herself has been justly criticised for this approach being 'too general' (Ringrose and Renold 2016: 221), its application in particular contexts may provide insights not only as to how certain movements are able to cause an effect, but also why they come to an end, or worse, become eaten and rebranded by the very machine they intended to dismantle.

In taking Braidotti's critique of becoming woman seriously and appreciating her post-anthropocentric conceptualisation of nomadic subjectivity, I demonstrate the utility of becoming-animal for becoming-woman. Important to this orientation is the reliance on experimental signification that, when deployed, immediately destabilises the environment the individual finds herself in, and thus the signification demanded of her. From this perspective, radical movements, such as the Riot Grrl movement in the 1990s, can be analysed through an apprehension of becoming-animal and used as a tool to open up onto becoming-woman. Braidotti (2014) also looked at the Riot Grrl movement in her article on the use of masks as a cultural and politic device amongst female musicians. Deviating slightly from this, I suggest that the participants in the Riot Grrl movement can be read as feminine subjects because of the territorialised space and bodies they find themselves in, as well as the use of feminine signification juxtaposed with becoming-animal to disrupt the biased and harmful codes of prescribed gendered subjectivity.

I. Becoming-Animal

In order to gain an understanding about how the feminine can be used to not simply transgress the capitalistic significations of femininity, but rather recode them as a means for revolutionary potential, a delineation of Deleuze and Guattari's concept of becoming-animal might be useful. The notion of 'becoming' is best understood as being aligned with Spinoza's philosophy of affect, illustrating a non-representational mode of thought (Tiessen 2012: 33). Deleuze and Guattari provide the example of the sun to further elaborate on becoming as affect:

> I feel the affection of the sun on me, the trace of the sun on me. It's the effect of the sun on my body. But the causes, that is, that which is my body, that which is the body of the sun, and the relation between these two bodies such that the one produces a particular effect on the other rather than something else, of these things I know absolutely nothing. (Deleuze and Guattari 1987: 256)

Deleuze follows Nietzsche in conceiving of the world as a series of productions, expressions and assemblages (Tiessen 2012: 34), and explores Spinoza's question 'What can a body do?' with the assertion that the body is composed of just such series. This is contradictory to many traditional psychological and humanist theories which conceptualise the individual as having a stable and unique core. Becoming in this sense is in direct opposition to being, and can be understood as modalities of being that are in constant experimentation, creation and disjunction. Such modes of being can take the form of a molar or molecular assemblage, which includes the materials and codes, or discourses, that compose it, but are also intertwined with one another (King 2012: 118). A molar assemblage has distinct edges and territories and is representational – what we traditionally identify as a stable identity, such as 'girl' or 'American'. Alternatively, molecular assemblages are those forces which animate the molar, as well as those forces which destabilise them. Molecular forces drive what assemblages come into being and can be referred to as open, dynamic, decoding and chaotic systems, in contrast to the codified molar systems (Deleuze and Guattari 1972: 182). While both the molar and molecular are mixed with each other in an assemblage, it is whichever one's properties are more abundant that determines the ultimate expression. Becoming then can be understood as a molecular process which is the constant process of one element of the assemblage linking with another, and the affect that is then produced. Becoming is inherently deterritorialising because it requires that the elements move from their original function and rather be momentarily constituted by affectation or influences. To deterritorialise is to make a move towards a body without organs, that is, a body with no organisational principles (Deleuze and Guattari 1972: 8). Deterritorialisation severs the word from its meaning; it scrambles the codes of signification. Deleuze and Guattari identify becoming-animal as having unique revolutionary potential (1987: 134). In her understanding of becoming-animal and becoming-woman as a means to move towards a corporeal feminism, Grosz explains that 'becomings are always a multiplicity, the movement or transformation from one "thing" to another that in no way resembles it' (1994: 173). Becoming-animal is not based on mimesis, resemblance or symbolic representations. Rather, becoming-animal involves a relation to something else, neither animal nor human, but something through which the subject can connect with the animal (Grosz 1994: 174). Becoming-animal is to enter into a molecular relationship with an animal. Deleuze and Guattari provide the following apparent methodological example:

> Do not imitate a dog, but make sure your organism enters into composition with something else in such a way, that the particles emitted from the aggregate thus composed will be canine as a function of the relations of movement and rest, or of molecular proximity, into which they enter. Clearly, the animal in question: it can be the animal's natural food (dirt and worm), or its exterior relations with other animals (you can become-dog with cats, or become-monkey with a horse), or an apparatus or prosthesis to which a person subjects the animal (muzzle and reindeer, etc.), or something that does not have a localizable relation to the animal in question ... we have

seen how Slepian bases his attempt to become dog on the idea of tying shoes to his hands using his mouth-muzzle. (Deleuze and Guattari 1987: 274)

In *A Thousand Plateaus*, Deleuze and Guattari explain how animals compose territories surrounding their body through different forms of expression, including posture, the use of colour, and song or establishment of a refrain (1987: 301–4). They emit and react to these expressive signs that become deterritorialised from original functions and reterritorialised within the context of their environment and interrelations therein. For example, a hawk flying over a given area can affect many potential prey below with its posturing, changing the nature of the environment while it is present. The multidirectional transformation (becoming) that is reflected in this process of deterritorialisation/territorialisation is relevant to how human beings can be transformed through expressive traits and affects as well, especially those of an entirely different nature than our own. To enter into a molecular relationship with an animal, to become-animal, then is to employ its affects, the various aspects of wolf-ness that makes a wolf or the snake-ness that makes a snake. In doing so, a body without organs is created through the collision with animal intensities, or that which determines the animal as different from human, and thus challenges the overdetermined nature of the body.

Feminist scholars have considered the potential analytical benefits of applying becoming-animal to issues pertaining to gender and equality. Renold and Ivinson (2014) uncovered the ways in which young girls in a community known for its equine history would use the horses to talk about gender and queerness. In doing so, they discuss the ways in which pure desire and becoming-animal in this context can be revolutionary and liberating. Similarly, though not focusing specifically on becoming-animal, Ringrose and Renold demonstrate how for young girls, sharing their experience of sexual objectification and feeling like 'cows' forms a 'discursive-material-physical sexuality assemblage' which 'connect(s) to a wider enduring historical and contemporary assemblage of becoming-meat' (2016: 227).

However, there are also valid hesitations that have been expressed with regard to this subject. Grosz clarifies that while it appears that becoming-animal advocates for a theoretical and political self-making reminiscent of liberal humanism, in actuality, becoming is not a matter of choice or a decision made on the part of the subject (1994: 174). This could be written back into the criticism that Deleuze and Guattari neglect the historical condition of women as struggling for subjecthood. Becoming-animal involves a substantial amount of subjective restructuring and can threaten the integration of the subject and social functioning. Needless to say, becoming-animal has the potential to be very uncomfortable because of its unpredictability. However, because of the weight placed on the affective potential, it has promise in its application for revolutionary work and counterculture practices, and in the same way in which becoming-animal challenges the over-determinedness of the body, it also can be utilised to reveal the arbitrary organisational systems as self-producing and potentially stagnant. Furthermore, when considered through the lens of feminist activism, it has the ability to challenge assumed codes about what constitutes a woman under patriarchal regimes of power.

II. Becoming Woman When the Woman Does Not Exist

As mentioned earlier, the feminine subject should not be thought of as someone who is essentially female or corresponds to a female body type, but rather a subject which fails to be fully accounted for in phallic signification. In order to fully understand this, Lacan's assertion 'there is no such thing as Woman' (1975: 72) must first be unpacked. By saying that woman does not exist, Lacan is not claiming that there is no female subject, but rather that the very act of entering language is inherently phallic. That is, language is a piece of ourselves that we can offer up to the Other as the cause of their desire, thus preserving our own sense of subjectivity, what Lacan refers to as castration. Feminine subjects, however, are unable to fully account for their desire in language and are therefore unable to become fully subjectified, leading him to assert that they must have an apprehension of outside of language. The feminine subject, then, is historically and socially contingent on the signifiers available, as well as held captive by them, such as the case of witches during the Middle Ages. It is worth noting here that Lacan and Lacanian feminist scholars have argued against an essentialised feminine subject, suggesting that the reason that the woman is more likely to be in the position of the feminine subject is due to socialisation, and that young boys, due to the presence of a phallus, are mistakenly socialised to believe that they actually have the cause of the Other's desire.

   This notion of the feminine subject is what allows Deleuze and Guattari to conceptualise becoming woman. They argue that all becomings must first pass through becoming woman, as it is 'the key to all becomings' (Deleuze and Guattari 1987: 277). For the purposes of my argument here, becoming woman can be understood as becoming not fully accounted for. However, as Braidotti suggests, in positing becoming woman as the means for all becomings to move towards a multiplicity while simultaneously calling for its dismissal, Deleuze attempts to bypass phallocentric representation on the promise of something new without properly contending with sexual difference as a metaphysical and epistemological difference (1994: 249). Furthermore, he fails to consider the double-bind of those subjects which must contend with the oppression of their sex, while also attempting to subvert essentialised assumptions about the sexes. Braidotti argues that because subjects find themselves within language, it might be beneficial to employ it strategically. She argues that when situated in hostile territory, it is crucial to gather those significations necessary for survival, specifically those that demarcate difference as opposed to ambiguity, until a safe place is reached to shed such limiting significations, what she refers to as nomadic subjectivity. Her theory is based on her own experience as a nomadic subject, in the sense that her European identity has provoked hostility depending on her location because of its potential ambiguity. In order to handle the hostility that this ambiguity provokes, she describes how she firmly roots herself in the appropriate nouns in order to continue moving through the territory, whether they be 'woman', 'Italian', 'Australian', 'academic', and so on. Braidotti seems to be advocating strategic rather than essential identification, yet this need to identify could also be seen as part of the problem, as women tend to get 'caught' in these molar constructions and thus become constricted by the very constructed paradigms that they need to assert themselves. This is why becoming-animal is crucial, especially in light of how easily these nominations ('feminism'; 'woman') can be appropriated. Braidotti's nomadism, coupled with Deleuze and Guattari's becoming-animal, provides insight into the kinds of strategies we must employ to move feminism forward.

For these reasons, I want to consider how those in the feminine position can deploy becoming-animal as a means to double back and deterritorialise those signifiers which claim to demarcate 'Woman'. In doing so, those subjects occupying a feminine position, within the safety of phallic signification, challenge that signification, not for the purposes of exchanging it for something else, which would also be inherently phallic, but to the point that the very contradiction is exposed. Woman as becoming-animal simultaneously demonstrates the impossibility of being woman, while also mobilising the potential latent in becoming-woman. Furthermore, I argue that the current instantiation of Woman cannot be separated from the capitalist commodification and that

Braidotti's nomadic subjectivity, through becoming-animal, provides a particular means through which to challenge the commodification of Woman, while also destabilising neoliberal capitalist subjectivity. To demonstrate this, I focus on the Riot Grrl movement in the early 1990s, Pussy Riot and FEMEN, to demonstrate the ways in which language, sounds and imagery evoke visceral experiences that rely on surplus affect that cannot be accounted for or signified. The tactics used by the Riot Grrl movement rely on playing with language and imagery to force their audience to experiment with their assumptions and fixed significations, specifically in relation to the molar feminine body. Furthermore, it is in the aforementioned examples, which I will elaborate on next, in which woman is a presumed essential category that needs to be first exited via becoming-animal in order to harness the potential of becoming-woman to challenge those assumptions and attempts at further phallicisation and commodification of 'woman'.

III. Becoming-Animal in the Riot Grrl Movement

The early 1990s saw the advent of the Riot Grrl movement. It was heavily influenced by the grunge and alternative scene at the time. In her book *Girls to the Front: The True Story of the Riot Grrl Revolution* (2010), Marcus explains how the movement initially began with singer Kathleen Hanna and drummer Tobi Vail. The movement centred around punk music, but more specifically, finding a place for women in the punk movement. It eventually became more than music and progressed to a feminist movement. Essential to the movement was an anti-capitalistic feminism, which emphasised reclaiming feminine subjectivity in a way that accentuated meaningful relationships between women, revolution and rebellion. The movement went beyond the music, and young girls and women met to discuss feminist issues, protest and write 'zines, as well as forming their own bands (Marcus 2010). In fact, Marcus explains that prior to forming Bikini Kill some members had never even played an instrument before. The music was an avenue for political expression.

When compared with the traditional discourses of femininity, the Riot Grrl's rebellious nature is revealed. In many ways the movement capitalised on a sort of grotesque, paradoxical femininity by taking what was considered gross or masculine and juxtaposing it with the baby-doll femininity of early childhood. For the purposes of this discussion, grotesque femininity refers to the practice or appearance that evokes an aversion or distaste because of the radical deviation from prescribed norms of femininity. Riot Grrls played with this aversion and radically changed the ways in which femininity could be expressed. Girls were refusing to shave their body hair or purchase products that would change or control their body odour. Combat boots were being worn with tutus, makeup was smeared or running, and their demeanour was loud, abrasive, serious and yet playful. Kathleen Hanna of Bikini Kill would frequently go topless in photos with the words 'slut' written on her chest, calling attention and provoking affective reaction to words that were being used flippantly to describe women. Her songs had similar 'shocking' themes which unapologetically and raucously referred to female sexuality and liberated embodiment (with titles such as 'Suck my left one', for example). She also arranged her concerts so that women could move to the front of the audience during her concerts and mosh safely without getting trampled by men (Marcus 2010). The fact that moshing is a type of dancing in which one engages her whole body and throws her head and hair around in an aggressive fashion contradicted the more demure or sexual dance moves expected of young women.

The grassroots Riot Grrl movements were also working to challenge patriarchal, capitalistic standards for femininity. For example, along with the 'zines, there was a movement towards 'radical menstruation', which rejected the notion that commodities were needed to sanitise a woman's menstrual flow, with the assumption that DIY products were more woman, and environmentally friendly (Marcus 2010). Such approaches called for a return to the 'natural' feminine body, challenging the practices advocating a distanced, hygienic and ascetic relationship to the body through the consumption of aptly named 'feminine hygiene products'. These practices blatantly exposed what constitutes the grotesque feminine and the hypocrisy inherent in prescribed notions of femininity.

In many ways, the Riot Grrl movement exemplifies a nomadic approach to subjectivity through becoming-animal and was perhaps as successful as it was because of these tactics. The strategies used in the movement also closely resemble becoming-animal. First of all, the movement rose out of the grunge and punk scene, a male-dominated genre. Just as animals deterritorialise and reterritorialise an area with sound, similar to how a wolf will howl to designate dominance and call to his pack or a crow will squawk to ward off other birds, bands such as Bikini Kill and Babes in Toyland used their sound to destabilise an area and recode it as a space safe for experimentation with femininity. Not only were these bands made up almost entirely of women, but their music was loud, obnoxious and vulgar, and anything but traditionally demure and feminine. Once this space was reterritorialised, Hanna would invite all of the women in the audience to move to the front of the stage (calling to the pack), enacting a literal reterritorialisation of the traditional grunge scene in which mostly men would mosh violently at the front, while women remained in the back (Marcus 2010). Furthermore, the type of dance elicited by such music allowed women to use their bodies in ways that allowed them to territorialise the space. By flailing limbs and headbanging, they take up more space, space generally dominated by their male counterparts. This is a demonstration of the ways in which posture is used in becoming-animal to recode an area, such as when a bird puffs up its chest or a spider will rise up on its hind legs. The bird, the spider or, in this case, the woman-becoming-animal claims space outside of her body which has a direct meaning and consequence for anyone or anything that enters this space. This type of reterritorialisation was not limited to the concert venue and spilled out into the rooms, cars, parties and a variety of other spaces inhabited by young women.

The greater historical context of the punk and grunge scene is particularly important when discussing the deployment of signs as a means of remapping. Signs are imitations which direct one to the thing which is being signified and have been used and exchanged for as long as there has been language. However, according to Baudrillard (1981), capitalism further removes signs from the original object which they were a supposed imitation of by emptying them of their meaning and recoding them in relation to capital, by hinting at something attainable beyond the copy, an ideal or actualised desire. However, this too is a copy, and an economy of signs is thus deployed using copies of copies referred to as simulacrum. Because of this relationship to reality, any emergent politics must account for this pairing of sign, code, capital and desire. In many ways, the Riot Grrl movement was aware of this exchange of signifiers and capitalised on it for their own means. They took those signs which signified anti-establishment and recoded them with feminist signification. They then deployed them in an arena that was both already familiar with these signs but was also guilty of hypocrisy in the exchange of them. The same people who were profanely deriding the government for its oppressive practices were confronted with their own systematic oppressive tendencies towards women in their perceived ideological sacrosanct territory.

IV. Commodification/Domestication of Becoming-Animal

As mentioned earlier, the ways in which the Riot Grrl movement affected traditional notions of the feminine, and thus feminine subjectivity, is more interesting for the purposes of this article than why it failed. However, in order to clearly follow the trajectory of the theory of nomadic subjectivity, times when the movement became ensnared are also important. For Braidotti, the risk of nomadic subjectivity comes when the subject becomes too identified with her nominalisations or significations and becomes static (1994: 64). Rather than apprehending the context in which one finds oneself and utilising those signifiers, one becomes 'woman' or 'Riot Grrl' in all contexts and forecloses on the potential offered by the space the subject inhabits. These identity markers are then trapped in signification and before long, recoded by capitalism as a commodity, and thus stripped of their subversive potential.

In Sini Anderson's film about Bikini Kill, *The Punk Singer* (2013), Kathleen Hanna remarks that one of the biggest reasons she believes that the Riot Grrl movement fizzled out was because it did in fact become commodified. 'Girl power' became packaged and sold to young girls through commodities, and bands such as Bikini Kill and Babes in Toyland were replaced by acts such as The Spice Girls and All Saints. Girl power moved away from DIY projects and was replaced by camouflage-coloured pencil cases, shirts, platform shoes, and so on, all emblazoned with GIRL POWER in pink glitter. The Spice Girls were marketed as identities that every little girl could adopt through the consumption of commodities, such as the sporty one or the glamorous, posh one. The 'girl power' signs that the Riot Grrl movement was playing with as a means to trouble the problematic feminine-woman signification were being copied once more and emptied of their prior signification. As Baudrillard explains, late-stage capitalism is now a system based on the signifier signifying the signifier, and the signified is further abstracted from the signs (1981: 164). In this case, the commodity signifies girl power rather than literal acts of girl power signifying the woman. This removes the subversive potential that was inherent in the deployment of girl power signification during the Riot Grrl movement because it no longer has the potential to destabilise capitalistic and phallocentric coding of the feminine. From the perspective of Braidotti's nomadic subjective, the Riot Grrls failed to move on when the territory was no longer fruitful, in the same way a nomad would. Rather, they clung to those significations that were once useful as if they were signifying what was actual, and what was once an act of fluidity became static and predictable.

V. Pussy Riot and Contemporary Politics

The Riot Grrl movement may have lost popularity, but it still finds representation online in forums, Instagram posts and blogs. It has also spawned its own revolutionary offspring, such as FEMEN and the band Pussy Riot. While these groups may not always directly credit the early 1990s movement, their tactics echo the early DIY approaches of the Riot Grrls and Guerrilla Girls (Art Scene Athens 2017). In looking first at Pussy Riot, what is of particular interest for this group is that their protests largely take place in areas that are dominated by traditional, conservative values, such as Russia, in which capitalism has not embodied the surplus enjoyment for everyone motto. While feminist paraphernalia have become money makers in the United States, with posters, hats, t-shirts, bags and coffee mugs printed with slogans such as 'Smash the Patriarchy', 'My Body My Choice' or 'This is what a feminist looks like', allusions to bodily autonomy or reproductive rights in authoritarian countries such as Russia are grounds for prosecution. Kirill, the head of the Orthodox Church in Russia, has gone as far as to say that feminism could destroy Russia (Elder 2013).

Because of this risk, one could surmise that Pussy Riot's subversive tactics maintain a disturbing urgency that has become muted in contemporary American feminism, in large part due to the commodification of the movement and the pacification of politics through the desire for capitalist consumption – you can have your cake and eat it too. Pussy Riot's protests on the other hand engage in ways that are difficult to reduce to a form-fitting t-shirt. Their music is independently produced, and their projects are crowdfunded (Cook-Wilson 2017). Furthermore, their protests do not rely on commodities or slogans, but rather appreciate the context and assault the sensibilities. For example, Pussy Riot's 2012 performance of 'Punk Prayer' in the Cathedral of Christ the Saviour in Moscow was infamously disruptive and controversial. In protest at Vladimir Putin's discriminatory and dictatorial policies, they donned bright clothing, stormed the cathedral and defiantly sang lyrics such as 'Shit! Shit! The Lord's Shit!' (MacDougall 2013). Without the neoliberal discourses to accompany these acts, they do not risk the same co-optation in the name of individuality, uniqueness or empowerment, and therefore remain at the level of the disruptive and disturbing. Even if the majority of the Russian people supported the protest, it is unlikely that they would endorse 'Shit! Shit! The Lord's Shit!' as a rallying cry. Finally, Pussy Riot reject conventional political tactics and events, and instead engage with a great deal of nomadism, moving throughout Europe and disrupting in contextually contingent ways, with everything from theatre productions (Cook-Wilson 2017) to unsanctioned (guerrilla-tactic) performances, outrageous performance art using explicit and shocking language and content, expansion to political activism for prisoners' rights, blogging, viral videos, as well as a number of other mediums for their projects. Furthermore, what is particularly important to their form of activism is that it is leaderless, in that anyone can be part of Pussy Riot, something they have articulated publicly (Kedmey 2014). Their use of masks destabilises notions of individuality, or activism as a form of identity politics. Instead, it allows anyone to join their pack and deploy their signifiers in contextually significant ways.

FEMEN is another a radical feminist group which operates outside of what might be considered safe or comfortable parameters of public discourse. Based in Paris but active across Europe, they describe themselves as fighting against the patriarchy in its three manifestations: sexual exploitation of women, dictatorship, and the imposition of religious institutions in the civic, sex and reproductive lives of women (FEMEN 2017). They are well known for their provocative public statements and strategic use of nudity ('Our Weapon [sic] are bare breasts!') to bring attention to political injustices and humanitarian issues, offering a pointed explanation of their mindset concerning their use of sexuality and the body: to 'turn your body against this injustice, mobilizing every body's cell to struggle against the patriarchy and humiliation' (FEMEN 2017). One such protest was staged in the Notre Dame Cathedral, where a FEMEN activist posed topless with the words 'May Fascists Rot in Hell', one day after Dominque Venner, a far-right historian and essayist, committed suicide in the same church (Willsher 2013). They also launched a 'Topless Jihad' in 2013 in support of Tunisian activist Amari Tyler, who, following an online post that featured her naked body with the words 'I own my body: it's not the source of anyone's honor', provoked the Commission for the Promotion of Virtue and Prevention of Vice to call for her to be stoned to death (Taylor 2013). They describe their ideology as a mix of feminism, atheism and sextremism: 'female sexuality rebelling against patriarchy and embodied in the extremal political direct-action events' (FEMEN

2017). They advocate for nonviolent, but highly aggressive, forms of provocation, premised in 'woman's mockery of vulgar male extremism and its bloody mayhems and cult of terror' (FEMEN 2017).

What makes Pussy Riot and FEMEN interesting for those interested in becoming-animal and becoming-woman is that their acts utilise animal signification without mimicking animals themselves. They rely on their bodies to communicate, using sounds, colours, and posturing to signify and disrupt. More importantly, they used the overdetermined female body to subvert the phallically organised space they find themselves in, and thus simultaneously challenge that very same female body. The loud, reverberating chants of Pussy Riot's music echo those of animals alerting their pack, calling them forth and signalling to their prey and hunters that they are greater in numbers and threatening. FEMEN with their bare breasts, refusing to don the significations that would render them a particular instantiation of woman as feminine or sex object, instead evoke primal associations to the body that births and feeds. The vulgar words written on their bodies, juxtaposed against this primal body, undermine any nurturing association, and further evoke a becoming-animal in the sense that it is the body that will bite back. Furthermore, it is important to note here that sextremism and its use to combat 'vulgar male extremism' threatens the (mis)recognition that man possesses the phallus. In following the Lacanian line of thought regarding feminine sexuation, it is that which is not fully castrated, which has caused some scholars such as Kristeva (1980) and Creed (1993) to posit that female sexuality threatens man's castration, and thus his subjectivity – it threatens to consume him. In doing do, FEMEN produces a schism between what woman is believed to be, and what the body of the woman can do. In becoming-animal, they retroactively open up becoming-woman and scramble those significations that have trapped the becoming-woman in the molar woman.

VI. Conclusion

Both the Riot Grrl movement and contemporary groups like Pussy Riot and FEMEN demonstrate how becoming-animal disrupts traditional codes of femininity. The Riot Grrl movement could be said to have engaged with becoming-animal with their screams and howls, not to mention body hair, in a further disruption of the notion of 'Woman'. However, the movement's inability to remain nomadic, and subsequently its commodification, demonstrates both the importance for this method of political engagement, as well as its potential for contemporary feminist politics. However, it is not the acts of revolt, but rather the crystallisation of identity and subjectivity in those revolts that allows for their capture and recoding. Contemporary groups, such as Pussy Riot and FEMEN, have demonstrated the importance of engaging with a nomadic politics that recognises and respects the unique constellation of factors in a given territory, making political engagement both complex, but also radically effective.

Note

1. Gray is the author of *Bad Feminist* (2014); Levy is the author of *The Rules Do Not Apply* (2017) and *Female Chauvinist Pigs: Women and the Rise of Raunch Culture* (2006).

References

Art Scene Athens (2017) 'Art Talks: From Guerilla Girls to Pussy Riot and Beyond', *Art Scene Athens*, 17 March, available at < https://artsceneathens.com/2017/03/10/art-talks-from-guerrilla-girls-to-pussy-riot-and-beyond/ > (accessed 10 July 2018).

Baudrillard, Jean (1981) *Jean Baudrillard, Selected Writings*, ed. Mark Poster, Stanford, CA: Stanford University Press.

Braidotti, Rosi (1994) *Nomadic Subjects: Embodiment and Sexual Difference in Contemporary Feminist Theory*, New York: Columbia University Press.

Braidotti, Rosi (2003) 'Becoming Woman: Or Sexual Difference Revisited', *Theory, Culture & Society*, 20:3, pp. 43–64.

Braidotti, Rosi (2014) 'Writing as a Nomadic Subject', *Comparative Critical Studies*, 11:2–3, pp. 163–84.

Cook-Wilson, Winston (2017) 'Pussy Riot Crowdfund an Autobiographical Theatre Production in London', *Spin*, 24 July, available at < https://www.spin.com/2017/07/pussy-riot-autobiographical-theater-piece-london/ > (accessed 13 July 2018).

Creed, Barbara (1993) *The Monstrous-Feminine: Film, Feminism and Psychoanalysis*, New York: Routledge.

Deleuze, Gilles and Félix Guattari (1972) *Anti-Oedipus: Capitalism and Schizophrenia*, trans. Robert Hurley, Mark Seem and Helen R. Lane, London: Penguin Books.

Deleuze, Gilles and Félix Guattari (1987) *A Thousand Plateaus: Capitalism and Schizophrenia*, Minneapolis: University of Minnesota Press.

Elder, Miriam (2013) 'Feminism Could Destroy Russia, Russian Orthodox Patriarch Proclaims', *The Guardian*, 9 April, available at < https://www.theguardian.com/world/2013/apr/09/feminism-destroy-russia-patriarch-kirill > (accessed 10 July 2018).

FEMEN (2017) 'About Us', *FEMEN*, available at < https://femen.org/about-us/ > (accessed 13 July 2018).

Grosz, Elizabeth (1994) *Volatile Bodies: Towards a Corporeal Feminism*, Bloomington: Indiana University Press.

Kedmey, Dan (2014) 'Those Two Pussy Riot Women? They're Not Actually in the Band Anymore', *Time*, 7 February, available at < http://time.com/5570/those-two-pussy-riot-girls-theyre-not-actually-in-the-band-anymore/ > (accessed 10 July 2018).

King, R. D. (2012) 'Molar/olecular', in Rob Shields and Mickey Vallee (eds), *Demystifying Deleuze: An Introductory Assemblage of Crucial Concepts*, Ottawa: Red Quill Books, pp. 117–19.

Kristeva, Julia (1980) *Powers of Horror: An Essay on Abjection*, New York: Columbia University Press.

Lacan, Jacques (1975) *On Feminine Sexuality, the Limits of Love and Knowledge, 1972–1973*, New York: W. W. Norton.

Lacan, Jacques (2007) *Écrits*, trans. Bruce Fink, New York: W. W. Norton.

MacDougall, Scott (2013) 'Pussy-Riot + The Orthodox Church = It's Complicated!', *Huffington Post*, 6 June, available at < https://www.huffingtonpost.com/scott-macdougall/pussy-riotrussian-orthodox-church-its-complicated_b_3397674.html > (accessed 10 July 2018).

Marcus, Sara (2010) *Girls to the Front: The True Story of the Riot Grrl Revolution*, New York: Harper Perennial.

Renold, Emma and Gabrielle Ivinson (2014) 'Horse-Girl Assemblages: Towards a Post-Human Cartography of Girls' Desire in an Ex-Mining Valley Community', *Discourse: Studies in the Cultural Politics of Education*, 35:3, pp. 361–76.

Ringrose, Jessica and Emma Renold (2016) 'Cows, Cabins and Tweets: Posthuman Intra-active Affect and Feminist Fire in Secondary School', in Carol Ann Taylor and Christina Hughes (eds), *Posthuman Research Practices in Education*, London: Palgrave Macmillan, pp. 220–41.

Taylor, Alan (2013) 'Femen Stages a "Topless Jihad"', *The Atlantic*, 4 April, available at < https://www.theatlantic.com/photo/2013/04/femen-stages-a-topless-jihad/100487/ > (accessed 10 July 2018).

The Punk Singer, film, directed by Sini Anderson. USA: IFC Midnight, 2013.

Tiessen, Michael (2012) 'Becoming', in Rob Shields and Mickey Vallee (eds), *Demystifying Deleuze: An Introductory Assemblage of Crucial Concepts*, Ottawa: Red Quill Books, pp. 33–6.

Willsher, Kim (2013) 'Femen Protester Stages Mock Suicide in Notre Dame Cathedral', *The Guardian*, 22 May, available at < https://www.theguardian.com/world/2013/may/22/femen-mock-suicide-notre-dame > (accessed 10 July 2018).

Litany on Forgiveness

This is where I live and breathe and write from, she said:
Forgiveness. This is the Jesus place, I thought,
suspicious of the banality but friendship had unleashed
the space.

This is the place of incarnation
where Yin fucks Yang
and scorn piggy-backs on those who seek love
but know not how.

This is the place where truth horrifies
and remains: Loss licks the brain like puppy's zeal
—giving and giving and giving until you cannot but give in
to the dream where you adore
torturers.

This is the place of humanity
where fathers become men
And mothers lay madness down
at their daughter's feet. Children must learn
to parent themselves.

This is the place of integrity where you refuse
to condone those who show their wounds by inflicting them.
Instead you become
she, awake in wide-eyed sweat,
who does not hunger for the fear of others.

This is the place of sanctuary,
where the wounded rests in honor and sings her wound
instead of staying powerless and sending offenders the bill.

The place where you,
kin to evil
and infinity,
matter.

Original poem by Valentine Moulard-Leonard,
Novelist and Philosopher

Deleuze and Guattari Studies 12.4 (2018): 523
DOI: 10.3366/dlgs.2018.0328
© Valentine Moulard-Leonard
www.euppublishing.com/dlgs

Gilles Deleuze and Donna Haraway on Fabulating the Earth

Aline Wiame   Université Toulouse–Jean Jaurès

Abstract

Inspired by Ursula Le Guin's 'The Carrier Bag Theory of Fiction', contemporary feminist writing in the social sciences and the humanities has been characterised by a strong renewal of interest in storytelling, as is evidenced by the works of Anna Tsing and Donna Haraway among others. How can storytelling grow with and beyond its literary origin to become a political and heuristic tool? And how does the Anthropocene – our specific geologic epoch – require the renewal of the means of expression of such an old tool as storytelling, so that it becomes a human and nonhuman process? To answer those questions, Deleuze's and Haraway's takes on 'fabulation' are intermingled along three lines: the part played by storytelling in the construction of earthly knowledges, the imbrication of speculation and politics, and the nonhuman dimension of fabulation that allows for the liberation of forces of life repressed by an anthropocentric approach.

Keywords: Anthropocene, fabulation, geophilosophy, Donna Haraway, Ursula K. Le Guin, Anna Tsing

I. Introduction: Feminist Storytelling against the Killer Story

The Anthropocene and the theoretical changes it has brought into the field of the humanities and social sciences have had an important impact not only on the concepts used but also on the writing styles and practices that this new geological epoch requires to be thought thoroughly. One of the defining traits of those writing styles and practices can be located

Deleuze and Guattari Studies 12.4 (2018): 525–540
DOI: 10.3366/dlgs.2018.0329
© Edinburgh University Press
www.euppublishing.com/dlgs

in a renewal of interest in storytelling, notably in the chief of feminist scholars. One can think of Donna Haraway (2016), Isabelle Stengers (2015), and Anna Tsing (2015). All three of them have a major reference in common when it comes to articulating stories based on feminist insight: fantasy writer Ursula Le Guin and her text 'The Carrier Bag Theory of Fiction', first published in 1986. In this text, Le Guin begins with the usual story of the 'Ascent of Man', a story that frames the origins of humanity as a hunting epic, with its Hero (usually a man), its fights, its killings, its linearity, and its goals both triumphant and tragic. Such a story, Le Guin argues, forgets that the first humans were actually hunter-gatherers and that the gathering part was the most important, the most sustainable. Maybe picking oats has nothing heroic in itself but picking up food and other things allows for a lot of free time – time to tell stories. Le Guin writes:

> It is the story that makes the difference. It is the story that hid my humanity from me, the story the mammoth hunters told about bashing, thrusting, raping, killing, about the Hero ... The killer story ... The trouble is, we've all let ourselves become part of the killer story, and so we may get finished along with it. Hence it is with a certain feeling of urgency that I seek the nature, subject, words of the other story, the untold one, the life story. (Le Guin 1996: 152–3)

Opposing the killer story to the life story also means opposing the hero story to the carrier one. What if stories were made of things picked up, and moved, and reorganised? It may be more difficult to write; it may be less suspenseful. But it also may be the only kind of story that can go on when the killer story has destroyed everything else. For Le Guin, this 'carrier bag theory' mostly applies to fiction (and, more specifically, to science fiction). But the beauty of the word 'story' is that stories can be fiction or not. You can make up stories but you can also tell true stories.[1]

Tsing's book, *The Mushroom at the End of the World*, is a remarkable example of this use of 'true' life stories that imply picking up and carrying many elements, human and nonhuman, to talk about the earthly condition imposed by the Anthropocene. The main subject of the book is the *matsutake*, a mushroom of high financial and sentimental value in Japanese culture. Tsing tells many stories to deploy the multiple connections between humans, landscapes, and mushrooms – stories of soils devastated by industrial exploitation (those are the best milieu for the *matsutake* to grow), stories of Asian-American war survivors who chose a marginal life picking up mushrooms in Oregon's forests, stories of the various stages of Marxist alienation a nonhuman – a mushroom, in this case – can endure. Those stories, for Tsing, are not mere examples; they are a way to think and to increase knowledge. She states early in the book that listening to and telling a rush of stories is a science, an addition to knowledge whose 'research object is contaminated diversity [and whose] unit of analysis is indeterminate encounter' (Tsing 2015: 37).

What would be the characteristics of such stories aimed at resisting the killer story and developing the life story? In a recent talk given in Paris, Didier Debaise mentions two important defining traits (Debaise 2017). First off, he argues, storytelling requires what William James calls an 'ambulatory' conception of thought, as opposed to a 'saltatory' one. A saltatory relation to the construction of knowledge consists in 'jumping' from one concept to another, thus erasing the distance, the steps, and all the singularities and possibilities that lie in the middle between two well-constructed concepts. But our true experience is always ambulatory, made of intervening parts through which one ambulates in succession (James 1909: 138). Storytelling is a way to resist the too disconnected, too badly constructed abstractions that poison an exclusively saltatory approach; stories follow the experience as it is constructed, step by step, along the path of the gatherer-carrier, of the mushroom picker. The importance of the ambulatory approach is reinforced by Debaise's second defining trait: the beings at stake in storytelling are always in a situation of precarity. As every being could very well not have been and could very quickly disappear, an ambulatory experience tries to explore every possibility, every singularity surrounding the beings persisting in their precarity. Moreover, precarity indicates the state of co-dependency, of reciprocal vulnerability, between every being, human and nonhuman. Although this co-dependency has always existed and must be considered as solidly as every other ontological feature, it is accentuated in the light of the perils brought by the Anthropocene, as Tsing underlines:

> What if, as I'm suggesting, precarity is the condition of our time – or, to put it another way, what if our time is ripe for sensing precarity? What if precarity, indeterminacy, and what we imagine as trivial are the center of the systematicity we seek? (Tsing 2015: 20)

We now have a first approach to storytelling as an addition to knowledge that defends an ambulatory process and takes precarity, indeterminacy, as its object. How can such storytelling grow with and beyond its literary origin to become a political and heuristic tool? And how does our specific geologic epoch require the renewal of the means of expression of such an old tool as storytelling, so that it becomes a human and nonhuman process? To answer those questions, I suggest we turn to Deleuze and Haraway, who have both – and independently – developed a theory of storytelling under such an intriguing name: fabulation. By bringing Deleuze and Haraway together around fabulation, my aim is not to correct or criticise one with the other but rather to determine how fabulation – and its particular relation with the question of the earth – can bring new elements in the carrier bag theory of storytelling. In essence, this is to align their views in a productive becoming. To do so, I shall first examine how the concept of fabulation is developed by Bergson, Deleuze, and Haraway in connection to specific peoples and to a singular link to what is or may be. I will then analyse how the question of the earth – of 'geophilosophy' – repositions fabulation in the context of the Anthropocene.

II. Bergson, Deleuze, Haraway: Fabulation as Inventions of the Unknown

The word 'fabulation' was brought into philosophy by Henri Bergson in *The Two Sources of Morality and Religion*. When he introduces the concept of 'fabulation function', he uses a case that could directly connect with what Deleuze will see in the concept: fabulation as an instinctive, imaginative act aimed at survival. A woman staying on the upper floor of a hotel is pushed back from the elevator that she was about to enter by a man working on the machine. The woman then realises there was no man and no elevator, even if its external door was open: she had 'fabulated' the scene as an instinctive coping mechanism quicker to make her react than a rational examination of the fact that she was about to walk to her death. As Bergson puts it:

> It was then that the instinctive or somnambulistic self, which underlies the reasoning personality, came into action. It had seen the danger, it had to act at once ... inducing in a flash the fictitious, hallucinatory perception the best fitted to evoke and explain the apparently unjustified movement. (Bergson 1935: 99–100/125)[2]

But that first introduction to what Bergson calls *fonction fabulatrice* can be misleading. His real aim is not to analyse individual survival instincts raised by the 'somnambulistic self' but to determine how myths and religions were born in the first human societies (which he qualifies as 'static' and 'primitive'). Human societies are organised by intelligence, Bergson argues, and intelligence has a dissolving power as it calls for individual initiatives that can put the social order in peril. As, in human societies, instinct is not strong enough to incite to action or to prevent it, it will have to provoke an illusory perception to counteract the corrosive powers of intelligence: 'Looked at from this first point of view, religion is then a defensive reaction of nature against the dissolvent power of intelligence' (Bergson 1935: 101/127). The fabulation function is thus a kind of ruse deployed by Nature to hold 'primitive', 'static' societies together:

> For the pressure of instinct has given rise, within intelligence, to that form of imagination which is the fabulation function. Fabulation has but to follow its own course in order to fashion, out of the elementary personalities looming up at the outset, gods that assume more and more exalted form like those of mythology, or deities ever more degraded, such as mere spirits, or even forces which retain only one property from their psychological origin, that of not being purely mechanical, and of complying with our wishes, of bending to our will. (Bergson 1935: 138–9/172–3; translation modified)[3]

Some defining traits of Bergson's concept of fabulation will be fought by Deleuze, explicitly or not. Firstly, fabulation, here, is a step in the moral and religious evolution of human societies; 'modern' societies, which Bergson calls 'open', do not need it anymore. Secondly, fabulation is a product of imagination that is constructed on the basis of *memories*. Thirdly, although Bergson recognises that novels and drama have recourse to fabulation, he states that 'novelists and dramatists are certainly not necessities; the fabulation faculty in general does not correspond to a vital need' (1935: 166/206–7).

When Deleuze, from the 1980s onwards, 'rediscovers' the concept of fabulation, all of those Bergsonian characteristics disappear, beginning with the supposed religious origin of fabulation. Deleuze claims a *political* approach to fabulation that includes the arts, and thus makes them necessities: 'it's more a question of a "fabulation" in which a people and art both share. We ought to take up Bergson's notion of fabulation and give it a political meaning' (Deleuze 1995: 174/235).

Actually, when Deleuze says so, he has already taken up Bergson's notion in *The Time-Image*, about political cinema. Fabulation is described therein as storytelling, an impersonal speech-act through which a people can invent itself, as it is 'missing'. The people is missing because the modern State associated with capitalism puts a stop to its individuation; the people is missing because colonisation has doubly subjected it, 'colonized by stories that have come from elsewhere, but also by their own myths become impersonal entities at the service of the colonizer' (Deleuze 1989: 217/283). But fabulation, a collective storying of and by the people itself that escapes the imposition of the truth of the powerful, disturbs this colonial attempt: 'The moment the master, or the colonizer, proclaims "There has never been a people here", the missing people is a becoming, it invents itself, in shanti towns and camps, or in ghettos, in new conditions of struggle to which a necessarily political art must contribute' (217/283; translation modified).

What can a people do when it has been suppressed by foreign stories, when its own stories have been emptied? For Deleuze, the answer must neither imply a preformed collective answer (the people being not there, any collective enunciation would be another usurpation of identity) nor a personal narration (since an addition of existing individualities does not constitute a people). Fabulation, in other words, is neither psychological nor collective. Deleuze thus defines fabulation as a kind of median voice: it is neither the singular voice of an author, nor the already defined voice of purely fictional characters. he writes:

> Fabulation is not an impersonal myth, but neither is it a personal fiction: it is a word in act, a speech-act through which the character continually crosses the boundary which would separate its private business from politics, and which itself produces collective enunciations. (Deleuze 1989: 222/289; translation modified)

The art implied here is not the art of an author; the authors – be they filmmakers or novelists – have to get themselves in a position that allows their real (and not fictional) characters to 'fabulate' – Deleuze also says 'legend-make' (*légender*) or 'make up fiction' (*fictionner*). Let us think of filmmaker Pierre Perrault who, in *Pour la suite du monde*, asked inhabitants of the island Isle-aux-Coudres (Quebec) to revive the long-abandoned practice of porpoise-fishing.

One thing should be clear here: fabulation has nothing to do with a formula to 'find' or 'locate' *the* people. The end of history when the true people will finally arrive is out of the equation, as Deleuze emphasises that the people to come can only be minor and multiple. About the end of the classical revolutionary paradigm, Deleuze writes: 'The death-knell for becoming conscious was precisely the consciousness that there was no people, but always several peoples, an infinity of peoples, who remained to be united, or should not be united, in order for the problem to change' (1989: 220/286; translation modified). That infinity of peoples is not even to be looked for on a strictly human scale, as Deleuze adds that 'if the people is missing, if it is breaking up into minorities, it is I who am first of all a people, the people of my atoms as Carmelo Bene said, the people of my arteries as Chahine said' (220/287).

At this point, one cannot help but wonder: why would Deleuze reuse the same word as Bergson while almost everything differs in their respective conceptions? Fabulation is not religious anymore but political; it is not confined in a specific moment of the evolution of human societies; it does not rely on memories as it is always turned towards the to-come; it needs art as a decisive tool rather than making it a harmless side-effect. Actually, the only common point that unites Bergson's and Deleuze's takes on the concept may well be the specific regime of production of truth fabulation delivers with real, social effects answering a vital need. In his lessons at University of Vincennes, Deleuze is pretty clear about that fact: 'Fabulating. It doesn't mean lying ... It means: legend-making. It means: getting caught red-handed. Getting caught for lying? No. Getting caught red-handed, that's the limit, that's the passage' (Deleuze 1985; my translation). Here, fabulation produces its own truth, as it is the process of fabulation itself that is the passage, connecting a character to its people, to what Deleuze calls its 'fabulous memory' (*mémoire fabuleuse*). Deleuze quickly refers to Bergson's fabulation function as the process of making a people come together, but this time on the basis of a memory that is fictionalised, fabulated:

> Yes, this people exists, but it exists outside of history, outside of the lived. Where does it exist then? It exists insomuch as it is invented; it goes both ways. How will it be invented? Fabulous memory. There is no history here – history is always the history of the coloniser. Fabulous memory ... it is crucial that there is no preliminary fiction. One must go, in an unsuspected way, from the everyday-life character lived as oppressed to the function of fabulation; one goes from the poor Indian to its fictionalisation, to its activity of fiction-making, and it is in this activity of legend-making that the reconnection to the people operates. (Deleuze 1985; my translation)

To describe the activity of this fabulous memory that is not based on history, I would like to quote an expression by Arthur Rimbaud that Janae Sholtz uses to describe Deleuzian fabulation: *inventions d'inconnu*, inventions of the unknown. Speaking of inventions of the unknown means that the unknown is not 'discovered' but that it can only be invented in a kind of fabulation regime, 'not predicated on a return to origins or a concept of truth' (Sholtz 2015: 228). Fabulation happens in-between; it does not occur as the myth of a past people, and it certainly does not occur as a positivist assessment. Fabulation refuses both fatalism and escapism in pure fiction. Fabulation is an addition to the reality it deals with – it makes potentialities appear and gives strength to the potentialities it develops.

This level of invention, which is neither true nor false but can produce true effects, is the best point to engage the discussion between Deleuzian fabulation and Haraway's own take on the concept. Beginning this discussion is difficult, as Haraway elaborates her own concept of 'speculative fabulation' without any reference to Deleuze – the choice of the expression comes primarily from a will to distinguish her kind of anticipative fiction from the broader literary genre of 'speculative fiction'. Before examining what is at stake in Haraway's choice of the wording 'speculative fabulation', it is useful to remember that storytelling has always been for her, at least since 'A Manifesto for Cyborgs', a powerful political and feminist tool:

> Cyborg writing is about the power to survive, not on the basis of original innocence, but on the basis of seizing the tools to mark the world that marked them as other. The tools are often stories, retold stories, versions that reverse and displace the hierarchical dualisms of naturalized identities. In retelling origin stories, cyborg authors subvert the central myths of origin of Western culture. We have all been colonized by those origin myths, with their longing for fulfilment in apocalypse ... Feminist cyborg stories have the task of recoding communication and intelligence to subvert command and control. (Haraway 2004: 33)

Multiplying stories and versions of origin stories is vital, as stories are tools of resistance and subversion. But the term 'speculative fabulation' itself only appears later in Haraway's work, when she directly reflects on the impact of climate change, beginning with the 2011 booklet *SF: Speculative Fabulation and String Figures*. Fabulation is introduced as a speculative device aiming to shape new ways of 'worlding' towards a speculative people called 'Terrapolis'. Speculative fabulation is thus born out of the radical shift imposed by the Anthropocene: because we need new worldings, new accounts of what we are making to and with the earth, we need speculative fabulation as 'multispecies storytelling, multispecies worlding' (Haraway 2011: 5).

Would speculative fabulation be a conceptual device to think the renewal of storytelling in the face of the Anthropocene? *Staying with the Trouble*, Haraway's last book, points convincingly towards that direction. The book has a whole chapter about Ursula Le Guin and Octavia Butler, and concludes on Haraway's own attempt at writing fiction – an anticipative short fiction entitled 'The Camille Stories: Children of Compost' (Haraway 2016: 134–68). But speculative fabulation is not only presented as a theoretical tool to talk *about* the world and its beings: if Haraway gives so much importance to speculative fabulation, it is because it is already part of what the world does. *Staying with the Trouble* at times suggests that storytelling and storying, are necessary components of the ongoingness of living beings, for instance when talking about 'companion species whose job in living and dying is not to end the storying, the worlding' (40). Here, 'storying' and 'worlding' are used as synonyms – storying is making a precarious world continue to exist.

While Haraway's frame of reference to introduce speculative fabulation does not include Deleuze's take on the term, some similarities are striking, such as the urge for survival and resistance to oppressive conditions of life and the necessity to compose with other beings in order to develop a fabulation that is not a personal question. Moreover, by suggesting that fabulation is 'speculative', Haraway also insists on the attention to hidden or disregarded potentialities that characterise a fabulation mode, joining Deleuze on the importance of storytelling for inventing the unknown and reasserting the importance of paying attention to the precarious conditions of life in our time.

However, Haraway's attention to the specific requirements of the Anthropocene also refines the depiction of the 'peoples' engaged in speculative fabulation. Quite obviously, her approach is multispecist and is not limited to human peoples. The peoples she pays attention to are also, literally, 'earthly': the importance planet Earth has taken in contemporary thought must be materialised in the full sense of the term, which means peoples interesting to Haraway are from the soil, from humus, from the underground. She emphasises how subversive versions of history produced by fabulation oppose the 'airy' myth of sunny *Homo sapiens* emerging from darkness: 'Terrapolis is of and for humus, the stuff of *gunman*, an old earthy Indo-European word for workers of the soil, not the stuff of *homo*, that figure of the bright and airy sacred image of the same' (Haraway 2011: 5). We are thus facing a conception of fabulation that not only requires storytelling for a people and an earth that are missing; the peoples engaged in fabulation are earthly *per se*, the passage that is fabulation being also a passage from an airy condition to an earthly one or, as Latour would say, from a human conception of history to *geohistory* (Latour 2015).

III. Geophilosophy and Resistance to the Present

If Haraway's approach to fabulation is directly embedded in the new climate regime and requires a strong connection between the peoples-to-come and the earth, this connection was already present in Deleuze and Guattari's philosophy. At first glance, fabulation seems primarily focused on a missing people but the people is not missing without the earth being missing too. The first occurrence of the theme of the missing people appears in the 'Refrain' chapter of *A Thousand Plateaus*, where it is connected to questions of earth and territory. And this interweaving of peoples, earth, and territory is, Deleuze and Guattari argue, a question and a struggle for the arts as well as for philosophy (1987: 342–7/422–8).

It thus comes as no surprise that this point is highlighted in the 'Geophilosophy' chapter of *What Is Philosophy?*, in an extract that brings together philosophy and art in a common task of creative resistance towards the invention of an earth and a people:

> We lack creation. We lack resistance to the present. The creation of concepts in itself calls for a future form, for a new earth and people that do not yet exist ... Art and philosophy converge at this point: the constitution of an earth and a people that are lacking as the correlate of creation. (Deleuze and Guattari 1994: 108/104)

There are at least two remarkable features in this quotation. Firstly, both art and philosophy are defined as creative – and thus subversive – activities (what I have suggested we call 'invention of the unknown'). Secondly, by positing that the constitution of an earth and a people that are lacking is the correlate of creation, Deleuze and Guattari implicitly bring fabulation at the centre of the process, as the invention of a people that is not there yet is the *function* of fabulation. Could it mean that fabulation is a central tool, both artistic and philosophical, to resist the present? Answering positively to this question implies to take into account the context of the quotation, which is geophilosophy. If fabulation can become a subversive tool, it is in a new, specific mode of thought that revolves around the earth and not the human subject. As Gregory Flaxman underlines, the passage from philosophy to geophilosophy totally changes the focus: 'Geophilosophy consists in nothing less than the resolution to situate philosophy in relation to inhuman *gaia* as opposed to inhabited *khton* – in other words, to make thinking a matter of the earth rather than a measure of the ground' (2012: 81). Flaxman later adds that, 'In discussing geophilosophy, then, we should bear in mind that the prefix "geo" (derived from *ge*) signifies precisely the deterritorialisation of thinking from its human regime (*gene*) – the "categories of subject and object" – onto the earth' (88), directly quoting from the first lines of the 'Geophilosophy' chapter, which say: 'Thinking is neither a line drawn between subject and object nor a revolving of one around the other. Rather, thinking takes place in the relationship of territory and the earth' (Deleuze and Guattari 1994: 85/82).

In the frame of geophilosophy, which tackles the problem of a missing earth and a missing people in the regime of inhuman *gaia*, fabulation takes on a whole new dimension as it does not concern only human oppressed peoples but also nonhuman beings and forces. When the concept of fabulation is mentioned in *What Is Philosophy?*, in relation to art, we can easily see clues to this shift. In the 'Percept, Affect, and Concept' chapter, fabulation is introduced as the act art does. A work of art, Deleuze and Guattari argue, is something that stands on its own, without the need to be animated by human psychology. A work of art is thus a bloc of percepts and affects, which by definition are nonhuman: '*Affects are precisely these nonhuman becomings of man*, just as percepts – including the town – are *nonhuman landscapes of nature*' (Deleuze and Guattari 1994: 169/160). As this bloc of affects and percepts, a work of art is a monument but not in the 'commemorative' meaning of the term, as it does not relate to the past or memory. How to express the action of the monument if it does not commemorate? The answer is fabulation: 'The monument's action is not memory but fabulation' (168/157). Indeed, 'creative fabulation has nothing to do with a memory, however exaggerated, or with a fantasy. In fact, the artist, including the novelist, goes beyond the perceptual states and affective transitions of the lived' (171/161). The artist, they continue, sees something bigger than life as it is lived by a human – a theme that was already present in Deleuze's lessons about cinema and thought where the people to come exists outside of the lived. But this time, inventing what is outside of the lived does not only concern human peoples and extends to the freeing of life itself: 'It is always a question of freeing life wherever it is imprisoned, or of tempting it into an uncertain combat' (171/162). Hence, characters created by fabulation are always 'giants', not born out of human memories and psychology but extracted from the forces of life: 'all fabulation is the fabrication of giants' (171/162; see also Deleuze 1997: 118/147).

We are already familiar with the fact that fabulation is oriented towards the invention of futures, of becomings, rather than towards the memories of the past. But one major element is new here: the action of fabulation gets further away from an exclusively human sphere – hence, correlatively, the choice of terms such as 'monument' and 'giant', underlining that fabulation directly operates at the scale of the forces of life. The partition of arts between affects and percepts also reflects this nonhuman becoming: affects and percepts, as the nonhuman becomings of respectively humanity and nature, mirror the 'unknowns' fabulation creates – a people on the one hand, an earth on the other.

For fabulation to get such an important part to play as a creative tool resisting the present, the new regime of thought that is geophilosophy, with its insistence on the forces of life that can never be captured by human forces, had to be in place. In this regard, *What Is Philosophy?*'s passages about fabulation echo some aspects of the 'Geophilosophy' chapter.[4] Let us turn, for instance, to Deleuze and Guattari's remarks about the reterritorialisation of contemporary philosophy on the State. Philosophy has felt the need to reterritorialise on the State, they argue, because it has lost its insertion into Nature. Mentioning Schelling, they write:

> Or, as Schelling put it: the Greeks lived and thought in Nature but left Mind in the "mysteries," whereas we live, think, and feel in the Mind, in reflection, but leave Nature in a profound alchemical mystery that we constantly profane. (Deleuze and Guattari 1994: 101–2/98)

The idea that we have mastered concepts but have lost 'Nature' – the earth – in the process clearly explains the part art and fabulation have to play in geophilosophy: by developing percepts that are nonhuman landscapes of nature, by extracting affects as nonhuman becomings, they set up a new earth for thinking on the mode of inhuman *gaia*. That mode of thought thus resists the present by liberating the forces of life: '[Books of philosophy and works of art] have resistance in common – their resistance to death, to servitude, to the intolerable, to shame, and to the present' (Deleuze and Guattari 1994: 110/105).

IV. Conclusion: Non-Innocence to Live and Die Well

Thorough this article, I have shown that fabulation cannot be reduced to a literary analytical tool and cannot be fully comprehended as a concept solely regarding the arts. Because it emphasises the passage, the continuous inventions of the unknown, fabulation is an intrinsically political process: fabulation refuses to locate its subjects in one formed identity, therefore resisting the solidification of emptied myths that rigidify places and positions and that subjugate their subjects. However, this political characteristic of fabulation does not cast the arts aside. As Haraway reminds us by equating 'storying' with 'worlding', fabulation is a part of what the world does, and thus artistic inventions of the unknown are required to maintain the ongoingness of living beings and their connections to nonhuman affects and percepts that were imprisoned.

Moreover, I argue that the interest for a process such as fabulation in the late twentieth and early twenty-first centuries has nothing to do with chance, as it echoes the need for geophilosophy – the deterritorialisation of thinking from its human regime onto the earth. One cannot grasp the double becoming that is being fabulated – a multispecific people and its missing earth – without recognising the radical regime change that is imposed on thinking by the eruption of Gaia (see Latour 2015; Stengers 2016). As this new 'geo' regime deterritorialises not only thinking but also affects and percepts, the strange epistemological status of fabulation (neither pure fiction nor positivist truth) becomes an asset for feminist writing in human and social sciences. The impossibility to assign fabulation to traditional categories of thought (true *or* false, human *or* nonhuman, abstract *or* affective) makes it a powerful tool to resist the killer story and develop life stories making room for an ambulatory approach to beings characterised by multilevel precarity and co-dependency.

In order to open those conclusive remarks to yet-to-explore paths for future ambulation, I would like to emphasise the necessity of keeping alive the discussion between Deleuze and Haraway regarding the philosophical status of fabulation. In Deleuze's (and Guattari's) work, the notion of fabulation gains the leverage of a concept that brings together art and philosophy and impacts the conceptual coordinates of the earth and its peoples. As a consequence, Deleuze's understanding of the earth is first and foremost philosophical: the new earth to be fabulated is an earth for and of thought.[5]

I suggest that this philosophical efficacy of fabulation must be both preserved and affected by Haraway's more materialist and feminist approach. The insistence she develops on the 'dirty business' of being earthly prevents all theoretical temptations to think of the earth as an ethereal entity, as a mere concept: dealing with the earth is dealing with humus, with the soil, with shady creatures from the underground – one has to remember that Deleuze and Guattari use the word *terre* in French, designating at the same time the Earth, land, and soil, this messy matter you can grasp with your hands.

Getting one's hands dirty when dealing with the earth is also a reminder that fabulation is not an innocent practice – actually, nothing that regards the current becomings of the planet and its peoples is. The non-innocence of our knowledges and practices has always been central to Haraway's work – think for instance of her work on the way we interact with dogs following interwoven lines of domestication, colonisation, control, and training (Haraway 2003). Her book title *Staying with the Trouble* indicates once again that we cannot evade the discomfort our interactions with other humans and nonhumans get us in. 'The Camille Stories', Haraway's own attempt at fabulation, describes such a situation of discomfort and of non-innocent choices in a close future when global warming and the sixth massive extinction of species accelerate. In Haraway's fabulation, human births are controlled (although not in an authoritarian way), endangered species die, practices of mourning are developed in cross-cultural manners between native peoples and the grandchildren of their colonisers – innocence has no place in such a world.

During a conference in Brussels in March 2017, when answering questions about 'The Camille Stories', Haraway developed on this question of non-innocence by saying that she was resolutely *not* pro-life. Obviously, she is not pro-life because she defends the right for a woman to have access to affordable and safe abortion procedures but, she added, her problem with pro-life thought goes beyond that issue. Wanting to associate life with sanctity, with purity, she argued, is a false position of innocence that negates the fact that life comes with cruelty, predators and preys, sickness and death. Stories of 'pure' life that negate that fact are myths of origins with politically dangerous consequences – those are stories that cannot fabulate plausible, liveable futures (Haraway 2017).

While Deleuze and Guattari are well aware of the non-innocence of our knowledges and practices, while they are very much conscious of the darkness that is inherent to the forces of life,[6] some of their expressions could lead a not careful enough reader to the conclusion that the 'forces of life', which fabulation seeks to free, are pure and ethereal, conceptual without being truly earthly. Haraway's resolutely materialist and feminist approach compensates for this imprudent reading, and invites us to revisit Deleuze and Guattari's passages about the non-innocence of life. In the Anthropocene epoch, fabulation is a political and non-innocent concept, as the stakes are no less than continuing the life story on an earth where it would remain possible to 'live and die well' (Haraway 2016: 1).

Notes

1. See Bogue 2010: 31, where Bogue draws parallels between the English word 'story' and the French word 'récit' – a word favoured by Deleuze.
2. Throughout, the second page reference refers to the French edition.

3. There is a quite constant pattern, amongst translators, to not keep the word 'fabulation' as is. Here, Bergson's translators went for 'myth-making', while several of Deleuze's translators used the term 'storytelling'. I chose to restitute the word 'fabulation'.

4. For instance, Deleuze and Guattari's will to emancipate fabulation from the religious origin Bergson assigned to it, reiterated in a note (1994: 230/162), echoes the separation between religious figures and philosophical concepts that is underlined in the 'Geophilosophy' chapter, as well as the atheism that would characterise philosophy (89–90/86–7).

5. The different figures of a new earth for thought throughout Deleuze's works are a dominant theme in Lapoujade 2017.

6. See for instance Deleuze and Guattari 1994: 107–8/103: 'We do not feel ourselves outside of our time but continue to undergo shameful compromises with it. This feeling of shame is one of philosophy's most powerful motifs. We are not responsible for the victims but responsible before them.'

References

Bergson, Henri (1935) *The Two Sources of Morality and Religion*, trans. R. Ashley Audra and Cloudesley Brereton assisted by W. Horsfall Carter, London: Macmillan [Bergson, Henri (1932) *Les Deux Sources de la morale et de la religion*, Paris: Presses universitaires de France].

Bogue, Ronald (2010) *Deleuzian Fabulation and the Scars of History*, Edinburgh: Edinburgh University Press.

Debaise, Didier (2017) 'Narrations spéculatives: Comment les récits composent-ils desmondes?', keynote presentation, *La Composition du temps? Prédictions, événements, narrations historiques*, University Paris Nanterre, 7–9 June.

Deleuze, Gilles (1985) 'Pensée et cinéma – cours du 05/02/1985 – 3', *La Voix de Gilles Deleuze en ligne*, uploaded by University Paris 8, available at < http://www2.univ-paris8.fr/deleuze/article.php3?id_article=304 > (accessed 31 July 2018).

Deleuze, Gilles (1989) *Cinema 2: The Time-Image*, trans. Hugh Tomlinson and Robert Galeta, London: Continuum [Deleuze, Gilles (1985) *Cinéma 2: L'Image-temps*, Paris: Minuit].

Deleuze, Gilles (1995) *Negotiations, 1972–1990*, trans. Martin Joughin, New York: Columbia University Press [Deleuze, Gilles (1990) *Pourparlers*, Paris: Minuit].

Deleuze, Gilles (1997) *Essays Critical and Clinical*, trans. Daniel W. Smith and Michael A. Greco, Minneapolis: University of Minnesota Press [Deleuze, Gilles (1993) *Critique et clinique*, Paris: Minuit].

Deleuze, Gilles and Félix Guattari (1987) *A Thousand Plateaus: Capitalism and Schizophrenia*, trans. Brian Massumi, Minneapolis: University of Minnesota Press [Deleuze, Gilles and Félix Guattari (1980) *Mille plateaux*, Paris: Minuit].

Deleuze, Gilles and Félix Guattari (1994) *What Is Philosophy?*, trans. Hugh Tomlinson and Graham Burchell, London: Verso [Deleuze, Gilles and Félix Guattari (1991) *Qu'est-ce que la philosophie?*, Paris: Minuit].

Flaxman, Gregory (2012) *Gilles Deleuze and the Fabulation of Philosophy: Powers of the False, Volume 1*, Minneapolis: University of Minnesota Press.

Haraway, Donna (2003) *The Companion Species Manifesto: Dogs, People, and Significant Otherness*, Chicago: University of Chicago Press.

Haraway, Donna (2004) *The Haraway Reader*, New York: Routledge.

Haraway, Donna (2011) *SF: Speculative Fabulation and String Figures*, Kassel: Hatje Cantz Verlag.

Haraway, Donna (2016) *Staying with the Trouble: Making Kin in the Chthulucene*, Durham, NC and London: Duke University Press.

Haraway, Donna (2017) 'Making Kin with Earthlings – Children of Compost, Read by Donna Haraway', Conference-reading, Centre for Fine Arts, Brussels, 31 March.

James, William (1909) *The Meaning of Truth*, London and New York: Longmans, Green.

Lapoujade, David (2017) *Aberrant Movements: The Philosophy of Gilles Deleuze*, New York: Semiotext(e).

Latour, Bruno (2015) *Face à Gaïa: Huit conférences sur le nouveau régime climatique*, Paris: La Découverte.

Le Guin, Ursula (1996) 'The Carrier Bag Theory of Fiction', in Cheryll Glotfelty and Harold Fromm (eds), *The Ecocriticism Reader – Landmarks in Literary Ecology*, Athens, GA: University of Georgia Press, pp. 149–54.

Sholtz, Janae (2015) *The Invention of a People: Heidegger and Deleuze on Art and the Political*, Edinburgh: Edinburgh University Press.

Stengers, Isabelle (2015) 'Science Fiction as Speculative Exercise', in Daniel Blanga-Gubbai and Lars Kwakkenbos (eds), *The Time We Share: Reflecting on and through Performance Arts*, Brussels: Mercatorfonds/Kunstenfestivaldesarts, pp. 366–72.

Stengers, Isabelle (2016) *In Catastrophic Times: Resisting the Coming Barbarism*, trans. Andrew Goffey, London: Open Humanities Press.

Tsing, Anna (2015) *The Mushroom at the End of the World: On the Possibility of Life in Capitalist Ruins*, Princeton, NJ and Oxford: Princeton University Press.

Queer Anomalies: Reading Contemporary Argentinian Literature

Francisco Marguch   New York University

Abstract

This article contrasts the identity politics that took place in the last decades in Argentina with the passing of the Civil Marriage Law and Gender Identity Law with the literary imagination of texts from the same years, in which sexuality exceeds categorisations and presents an anomalous horizon. The first part of the text examines Deleuze and Guattari's concept of the anomalous as a tool to redefine queer sexualities without recourse to a transcendental norm. The second part of the article looks at the work of two writers, Naty Menstrual and Pablo Pérez, as examples of the logic of the anomalous.

Keywords: anomalous, queer, Argentinian literature, sexuality, vitalism

I. Introduction

Argentina passed a Civil Marriage Law in 2010 and a Gender Identity Law in the year 2012, becoming, then, one of the most progressive countries in terms of LGBTQI issues worldwide. The passing of these laws required defining certain groups of people in terms of concrete, tangible, visible identities in order to become the subjects of the law. To enter into the legal universe and to access full citizenship meant performing for the State acts and speeches that made visible the struggles of part of the population. However, since the 1990s queer literature and arts have seemed to be going in the opposite direction. After a period that was also aiming towards visibility, of trying to define gay, lesbian or trans as terms of opposition to a norm, the State and heteronormative

Deleuze and Guattari Studies 12.4 (2018): 541–552
DOI: 10.3366/dlgs.2018.0330
© Edinburgh University Press
www.euppublishing.com/dlgs

culture, many artists and writers explored ways of thinking identity and sexuality as something more fluid, blurring the differences between what is normal and what is not. Without denying the unequal distribution of rights and the physical and symbolic violence that some bodies are exposed to while others are not, these fictions enacted ways of suspending the very same frames that produced those differences, rather than denouncing that violence.

Trying to understand the way that literature creates modes of perception that differ from the way that politics produces subjectivity, I read these texts though Gilles Deleuze and Félix Guattari's idea of the anomalous, arguing that this is a useful concept in redefining what being queer, strange, non-normative, non-conforming means without in the process forging a new identity. In this essay, I argue that the idea of the anomalous can reframe some of the main questions of queer theory by side-stepping the dualisms of normal/abnormal, centre/margin, heterosexual/homosexual and instead presenting an idea of sexuality and desire as a horizon of co-exceptionality, where everybody is susceptible to becoming queer. Thus, in this context, queer, more than an identity or a part of the population, makes for a virtual force.

The essay is divided into two parts: in the first, I explore Deleuze and Guattari's concept of the anomalous as a tool to provide an understanding of 'queer' as a vital force, rather than a reactive identity. In the second part, I reflect on the way in which contemporary Argentinian literature intervenes in the sphere of politics by presenting precisely difference as a queer potentiality of variation.

II. The Anomalous

In recent decades, *queer* became a name for groups of the population that escape the norm, whose bodies and desires interrupt the biopolitical demarcations of what a life should be. This has generated political, philosophical and artistic responses that could be characterised as antagonistic to that norm. However, Robyn Wiegman and Elizabeth Wilson point out that:

> in imagining the norm as a device that divides the world into centers and peripheries, antinormativity misses what is most engaging about a norm: that in collating the world, it gathers up everything. It transverses networks of differentiation; it values everything; it plays. (Wiegman and Wilson 2015: 17)

The problem with this politics of antinormativity is that it constitutes queer as a reactive concept, reinforcing an ontological primacy of the norm (and a social hierarchy of those who obey the norm) over what escapes it (and those who deviate from it).

By thinking about anomalies, we shift the focus from identity and the norm to multiplicities and borders, privileging the affirmative and transformative dimension of difference. While queer theory has mostly been rooted in deconstruction and philosophies of language, it can be argued that the thinking of Gilles Deleuze and Félix Guattari is more a philosophy of nature. Deeply informed by thinkers like Spinoza and Bergson, Deleuze's idea of difference has more to do with the immanent capacity of bodies to vary than with their ability to subvert cultural matrixes. To think about the concept of *life* and its biological component as a foundation for queer thinking can be a risky move, because it is also a concept that has had a very normative history. Nevertheless, this arguably makes it even more important to rethink the biology of life though non-normative lenses. Against a conservative form of vitalism, Claire Colebrook has found in Deleuze's work a vitalism of the virtual that she characterises as inherently queer, as it places a focus on the individual as something not given once and for all, but traversed by pre-individual intensities; a kind of vitalism that is not about the agency of a subject, but about micropolitics. She calls it *passive vitalism*, as a way to denote the characteristics that differentiate it from a vitalism that proposes to think about individual lives and volition:

> By understanding life as virtual we no longer begin with the image of a living body, and are therefore able to consider forces of composition that differ from those of man and the productive organism.... . Passive vitalism is queer, by contrast, in its difference and distance from already constituted images of life as necessarily fruitful, generative, organized and human. (Colebrook 2014: 100–1)

This passive vitalism focuses on difference and virtuality, potentialities and assemblages, rather than organised bodies and agency, understanding life as immanent. If we understand difference as something immanent and pre-individual, the question of non-normative desires and sexualities has to be re-evaluated in order to take account of a process of variation and differentiation irreducible to the individual. The mere gesture of adopting this kind of vitalism is itself politically interesting, as it contests the idea of life as an organised body that is given once and for all. The living is here always a force in a permanent state of change and variation, traversed by intensities that transform it continuously. Contrary to the belief that non-normative sexuality is a failed performance or a deviation from a norm, this passive vitalism sees the non-normative as the characteristic of life itself.

Interestingly, the term 'queer' that was used as a way of escaping rigid parameters of identity has become another term of self-identification. We can reconceptualise it as a vital force, not a part of a population based on their sexual practices. This meaning is closer to what Deleuze calls the anomalous, a category that can be useful in order to redefine queerness in a positive way and not as a negative response to a norm. This switch in our understanding of sexuality and difference is valuable, because it allows us to escape the ontological importance given to these norms, and rather to think of gender and sexuality as always susceptible to becoming anomalies, and as always being in relation to a certain queerness. Furthermore, rethinking the 'queer' in terms of vitality allows for an understanding of a queer materiality of the body. We can better understand a mandatory heterosexual matrix if we think about it as a response to the anomalous and the queer – material variations originating in a body's virtual potentialities – rather than if we imagine the queer as a subversion of the normal.

Deleuze and Guattari were particularly interested in Georges Canguilhem's definition of the anomalous, as found in *On the Normal and the Pathological* (published first as *Essai sur quelques problèmes concernant le normal et le pathologique*, in 1943). Canguilhem develops this concept taking from the distinction that André Lalande proposes in his 1927 text *Vocabulaire technique et critique de la philosophie* between anomaly and abnormal. The term 'anomalous' (in French, *anomal*) had fallen into disuse, but Lalande insisted on the etymological difference between the two terms:

> 'Anomaly' comes from the Greek *anomalia* which means unevenness, asperity; *omalos* in Greek means that which is level, even, smooth, hence 'anomaly' is, etymologically, *an-omalos*, that which is uneven, rough, irregular, in the sense given these words when speaking of a terrain. (Canguilhem 2012: 73)

The anomalous can thus be understood as a term in anatomy for cases of the unusual, the unaccustomed, but that nevertheless defines the broad possibilities of the species for generating difference. The idea is that the anomalous has to do more with degrees of variation within species than with a norm imposed externally. 'It is clear that, so defined, anomaly is, generally speaking, a purely empirical or descriptive concept, a statistical deviation' (Canguilhem 2012: 74). It does not, therefore, carry a moral or negative connotation. Conceptually, anomaly is far from the concept of disease, although some anomalies might develop into disease.

A Thousand Plateaus defines this concept as the exceptional position of an individual in a pack, and differentiates it from the abnormal, which would entail specific characteristics rather than a position in an assemblage:

> *an-omalie*, a Greek noun that has lost its adjective, designates the unequal, the coarse, the rough, the cutting edge of deterritorialization. The abnormal can be defined only in terms of characteristics, specific or generic; but the anomalous is a position or set of positions in relation to a multiplicity. (Deleuze and Guattari 2004: 244)

For Anne Sauvagnargues (2004), Deleuze and Guattari's philosophy of life and their theory of becoming propose a reframing of the relations between a singularity and its species, in which difference is redefined as an immanent variation and not through the application of an invariant transcendental norm. Also, the anomalous is not simply an exceptional individual in a collective, but a certain *lieu* in a multiplicity. In the words of Deleuze and Guattari: it is 'neither an individual nor a species; it has only affects, it has neither familiar or subjectified feelings, nor specific or significant characteristics'; it is 'a phenomenon of bordering' (2004: 244, 245), and, because of its condition as a border, it is also what enables becomings and the crossing of multiplicities.

Frida Beckman indicates that 'sexuality is seen as a stratified form of desire', and that unlike the other, it is deemed unproductive (2013: 6). Deleuze's own emphasis on desire versus sexuality and pleasure seems to go in this direction. In spite of that, Beckman argues that Deleuze's philosophy also enables a reading of sexuality as the virtual. Elizabeth Grosz, too, has offered a reading of Deleuze alongside Darwin's theories to elaborate a notion of sexuality as something creative, excessive, productive and incalculable. Sexuality is not a means towards the reproduction of the species, it is 'not about the production of a norm but about the eruption of taste' (2011: 130). For Grosz, difference – we might also say queerness – does not derive or deviate from the norm but is a product of the creative process that takes part in living matter. Living matter is therefore virtually queer by definition, because of its potentiality to vary.

Considering difference as a vital force and a bordering phenomenon can free us from the ontological derivations of making 'queer' a noun that refers only to certain bodies. This does not mean, however, that certain bodies are not more exposed than others to the violence of control by the State, Capital and cultural frames, but places the focus on the potentialities of borders and becomings, rather than in the hierarchical systems that attempt to limit these active forces.

In the next part of this paper, I will focus on some Argentinian literary texts that capture this understanding of life as inherently queer and that imagine a world of co-exceptionalities, and difference as a virtuality. These are texts that enable a reading of the micropolitics of difference that are not deeply rooted in identity, but that explore the anomalous borders of sexuality.

III. Literature and Its Borders

Marlene Wayar, an Argentinian trans activist and social psychologist, referring to the passing of the Gender Identity Law in 2012, says in the documentary *Conceptos en el corpiño*:

> Identity should be thought as 'what am I?' I'm being 'this'. I am *travesti*, I am trans, I am Argentinian. I have never been Argentinian, but went back to being that a few years ago. Argentina has invited us to be part of a discussion. Many concepts are in dispute, like what this nation is, and I, who have never been a nationalist in any sense and won't be, I want to explore that possible imaginary of being Argentinian.[1]

There is in this quote a temporary disjunction, a paradox. How can one go back to being what one never was? What is at stake here are two different senses of what belonging to a nation is. When she says that she was never Argentinian, she implies that the trans community was not represented by the state, was not recognised as an interlocutor. The crafting and passing of the bill, in which she and other trans activists and thinkers participated, meant a first gesture from the state towards the trans community. This 'going back' to the nation can be read as an assimilation to the state, but it could also be read as a minoritarian becoming, both of the people and the nation; a 'becoming anomalous'. Wayar's idea is interesting because it does not state that she goes from being completely outside the nation to inside it, but rather complicates notions of temporality and identity, as if the nation were just a virtuality.

This new chapter in Argentinian politics in which trans people, according to Wayar, are considered citizens and subjects of speech made visible their creative and intellectual work. Both the Civil Marriage Law and the Gender Identity Law were passed during the presidency of Cristina Fernández de Kirchner (2007–15), marking a new receptiveness of the Left and populist governments to gender and sexuality issues. Nevertheless, the Southern Cone region witnessed shortly thereafter a destitution of these progressive governments. In the case of Argentina, this was not through impeachment, like in the cases of Fernando Lugo in Paraguay and Dilma Rousseff in Brazil, but through elections that consolidated the right-wing candidate Mauricio Macri as the elected president in December of 2015. Suely Rolnik, a Brazilian intellectual who worked closely with Félix Guattari, points out that the contemporary landscape of Latin American democracies can be explained mostly through a new relevance of the concept of micropolitics. For Rolnik, financial capitalism takes power not through a military coup, but through the force of desire, 'a vital force that moves individual and collective existence' (2016: 3). A micropolitical strategy occupies now a central role in relation to the macropolitics of the State.

If literature works precisely with these pre-personal forces that are yet to be captured by the macropolitics of the State, reading some of the fictions produced in Argentina during that time might give us a clue as to what is in question in relation to this new relevance of the politics of desire. Rather than focusing on the split between language and reality and the dissemination of meaning, like some of his contemporaries, Deleuze sees in literature the possibility of creating and experimenting with new forms of life. If others saw in literature a hole, an abyss of language, Deleuze saw through this hole a traffic of affects, sensations, non-linguistic elements, colours and sounds. With this conceptualisation of literature in mind, I argue that there are some texts by contemporary Argentinian writers that present the invention of anomalous lives and that imagine sexuality not through a divide of normal versus antinormative, but rather through a regimen of co-exceptionalities. These narratives incorporate discussions of identity, but at the same time exceed it, as they register micropolitical differences and material variations of bodies. I will briefly discuss two examples that I think are representative of a larger group of texts that depart from a narrative that seeks to define a queer identity as antinormative, moving gradually to the terrain of micropolitics and a concept of difference that is not antagonistic, but based on the virtual potentialities of variation.

Naty Menstrual, a trans writer and performer, runs the blog *Naty Menstrual Blog 'Literatura Travesti Trash'*,[2] in which she publishes her literature. She has also published a collection of her short stories, *Continuadísimo* (2008), one of which is particularly interesting, entitled 'Butter Croissants': Marlene Brigitte is walking back home in the early morning after a night out, asking for spare change to buy a croissant she is craving, a very common breakfast in Argentina. She is tired of walking, she feels sore from the sex she had the night before, and she is nauseous from drinking. She gets home, freshens up, and after finding some money, heads out again to finally buy the croissants. She stumbles upon two young policemen. The story here plays with the reader's expectation that the police will probably interrogate her, based on the fact that *travestis* are a target of police abuse. Nonetheless, they flirt with her and they happen to have a bag of the same pastries she was craving. Marlene ends up having a threesome with them and then eating one of the croissants. The story chooses to suspend police abuse by imagining a sexual utopia with the police that fulfils the protagonist's sexual and culinary appetites. Rather than representing oppression in a direct way, this short story explores a heterogeneous alliance, a traffic of affects through social border, a universe of contagious co-exceptionalities and proliferating anomalies.

The second example is Pablo Pérez's first auto-fictional novel called *Un año sin amor* (1998) [A Year Without Love], which also has an alternative title, *Diario del SIDA* [AIDS Diary], it being precisely that: a fictionalised journal of an HIV-positive man at a time when the virus had stronger stigma attached to it. Estranged from his family, the narrator deals with the different drug cocktails needed to stabilise his body and a more general state of lovelessness, present in the title. A few years later Pérez published another auto-fictional book that can be read as a sequel to *Un año sin amor*: *El mendigo chupapijas* (2005) [The Cocksucking Beggar]. Despite the formal continuities (the hybrid journal genre, the same self-referential protagonist), this second text is largely a departure from the previous one in terms of the narrative that is being presented. We find the narrator enjoying himself through a series of sexual encounters, in a Buenos Aires that he describes as a place without norms, and in a period of his life characterised as a Spring, a Dionysian festival. Love here becomes more present, through an idea of 'universal love' that he takes from a healer he meets in France, which he experiences also in his sexual practices. Many parts of the book are devoted to him roving through the city, and towards the end, he passes by a beggar who is masturbating and who then leads him to an abandoned house with other beggars. He claims that this is the most luminous night of his life. He surrenders to them, as the last act of a process of becoming impersonal present all throughout the diaries. The project can be read as a deviation from a traditional narrative about HIV, from the first book to a second novel that focuses more on sexuality as an ethical exercise, as the possibility of experimenting with the plasticity of affects and body. Rather than construct a character based on a non-normative identity, the second text imagines a world in which the possibility of new encounters is endless and in which everyone is exposed to a queer virtuality.

In these two stories, each body is susceptible to becoming queer. There seems to be no outside of a shared affective regime or of an anomalous horizon. Queerness becomes then an intensity, something that happens between bodies, in their encounters, more than a specific demographic category. Queer seems to be a state of anomalous variation, instead of an identity. In an article about the possibilities of a queer theory deriving from Deleuze's idea of positive difference, Colebrook extracts the following aesthetic conclusions:

> Art would not be the representation or formation of identities but the attempt to present pure intensities in matter, allowing matter to stand alone or be liberated from its habitual and human series of recognition. The sensations presented in art are not those of the lived subject but are powers to be lived for all time, allowing us to think the power of perception beyond the selves we already are. (Colebrook 2009: 21)

These are literary pieces that focus precisely on those moments of suspension of identity and personhood, and shed light on worlds of encounters that actualise a pre-individual queerness. The issue here is not to deny a differential distribution of violence, but (like some of the fictions examined do) to imagine also a world of anomalous proliferations, of queer intensities that function as our ontology, and not as a mere opposition to the norm.

In this contemporary scenario, micropolitics and the pre-individual forces of desire seem to be at stake in both capitalist governments and queer communities alike, which, as in Wayar's quote above, seek to make a heterogeneous alliance with a Nation that tended to be rather exclusionary but that now displays new potentialities. The literary texts I have discussed do not present queer as an identity, but more as a shared horizon. They imagine bodies as inventive and expansive, while capturing in the process the economies of violence and the normative structures that try to control the wilderness of life. This sense of the word 'queer' is close to Muñoz's use of the term in *Cruising Utopia* (2009), since it highlights pre-personal potentialities over queer anti-relationality. Like in the story about the heterogeneous alliance between the *travesti* and the policemen, we can read in these narratives utopian temporalities. What I find interesting about the concept of the *anomalous*, however, is that these futures are localised in the materiality of life itself. It is in the living body where we find the potentiality of variation, the endless process of differentiation that is always relational.

IV. Conclusion: Literature, Anomalies and Becomings

Literature seems to be the terrain that explores the pre-personal grounds of this queer vitalism in the most interesting way. In a text from 1990 titled 'The Minoritarian Becomings', Argentinian writer Néstor Perlongher, an avid reader of Deleuze who in exile in Brazil met Rolnik and Guattari, already proposes something along these lines: minoritarian micropolitics that instead of crystallising rigid parameters of identity, tend towards the mutation of a production of subjectivity that becomes more and more serialised (2008: 73). He saw in the Southern Cone of the 1990s a crisis that was not only political and economic, but also a crisis of the 'modes of subjectification' that only a molecular revolution would avert. The invitation to think and to live in ways that escape the jail of identity, the utopian intensities disseminated in Perlongher's work during his exile after the Argentinian dictatorship seem to have a new relevance now, in a time when a conservative government was established not via a coup, but through democratic elections. And if the literary machines that Perlongher crafted invoked a molecular revolution, these fictions of the anomalous, too, seem to be doing just that: imagining new ways of life. Celia Palmeiro argues that many of the literary projects of the last two decades are deeply influenced by Perlongher's politics of the body, specifically by an explicit preoccupation with the interactions of literature and politics: 'Literature and politics are mutually enhancing: Literature as the imagination of possible ways of living, and politics as the art of transforming collective existence' (Palmeiro 2011: 17). Perlongher, who was not necessarily representative of the dominant trends of his times (too queer for the left, too left-ish for the gay movement that was emerging), seems now retrospectively an author deeply connected to some of the contemporary directions of Argentinian literature. Specifically, his concern with Guattari's concept of micropolitics and his exploration of minoritarian becomings through literature seem to resonate today.

After a cultural and political process of making identity visible and of defining modes of subjectivity, literature seems to be placing the focus now on the micropolitical: the lines of flight that escape these modes of representation and subjectivity. Sexuality then becomes creative by definition, since it is all about exploring borders, trafficking affects. In this scenario, anomalies become something shared, a community of exceptionalities, a vital force that pushes the body to go beyond itself.

In these projects, queer is a virtuality, a potentiality, that complicates the temporalities of a nation, as seen in Wayar's statement. The anomalous seems to act in a molecular level: not as visible as the antinormative, because of its instability, always on the border. Its politics are always micro: it is not about agency but assemblages. It does not define an identity but creates milieus of becoming. It does not refer to individuals, but sheds light on processes of singularisation. Its potentiality is encrypted in matter. Literary projects are particularly good at capturing this sense of the anomalous, since literature always works in the domain of the pre-personal, and therefore is capable of exploring what is happening at the borders.

Notes

1. Note that *travesti* is a term that many communities prefer in Argentina over 'trans', as it has a class connotation that links being trans with unequal access with economic resources and is often associated with sexual work. See Berkins 2013. The original quote in Spanish is: 'La identidad hay que pensarla como un "¿quién soy?, voy siendo esto". Soy trava, soy trans, argentina. No he sido argentina, pero desde hace algunos años he vuelto a serlo. Esta Argentina nos ha invitado a ser parte de una discusión. Están en disputa muchos conceptos, como qué es la patria, y yo, que no he sido nacionalista en nada ni lo voy a ser, quiero ver qué es ese posible imaginario de ser argentinos y argentinas ... Y qué va siendo.'
2. Available at < http://natymenstrual.blogspot.com > (accessed 5 December 2017).

References

Berkins, Lohana (2003) 'Un itinerario político del travestismo', in Diana Maffía (ed.), *Sexualidades Migrantes, género y transgénero*, Buenos Aires: Feminaria.
Canguilhem, Georges (2012) *On the Normal and the Pathological*, Berlin: Springer Science+Business Media.
Colebrook, Claire (2009) 'On the Very Possibility of Queer Theory', in Chrysanthi Nigianni and Merl Storr (eds), *Deleuze and Queer Theory*, Edinburgh: Edinburgh University Press, pp. 11–23.
Colebrook, Claire (2014) *Sex After Life: Essays on Extinction*, Volume 2, Ann Arbor: Open Humanities Press.
Conceptos en el corpiño, documentary, directed by Rocío Pichon-Rivière. Argentina: work in progress.
Deleuze, Gilles and Félix Guattari(2004) *A Thousand Plateaus: Capitalism and Schizophrenia*, trans. Brian Massumi, Minneapolis: University of Minnesota Press.
Grosz, Elizabeth (2011) *Becoming Undone: Darwinian Reflections on Life, Politics, and Art*, Durham, NC: Duke University Press.
Menstrual, Naty (2008) *Continuadísimo*, Buenos Aires: Eterna Cadencia.
Muñoz, José Esteban (2009) *Cruising Utopia: The Then and There of Queer Futurity*, New York: New York University Press.
Palmeiro, Cecilia (2011) *Desbunde y felicidad: De la Cartonera a Perlongher*, Buenos Aires: Título.
Pérez, Pablo (1998) *Un año sin amor*, Buenos Aires: Hoy x hoy.
Pérez, Pablo (2005) *El mendigo chupapijas*, Buenos Aires: Mansalva.

Perlongher, Néstor (2008) *Prosa plebeya*, Buenos Aires: Colihue.
Rolnik, Suely (2016) *A hora da micropolítica*, São Paulo: N-1 ediçoes.
Sauvagnargues, Anne (2004) *Deleuze: Del animal al arte*, Buenos Aires: Amorrortu.
Wiegman, Robyn and Elizabeth Wilson (2015) 'Introduction: Antinormativity's Queer Conventions', *Differences*, 26:1, pp. 1–25.

How Do You Live with a Bird for a Heart?

How do you forget the face of your criminal lover the way his voice
sang near water
the way his prison letters cut cuticles in the palm inside you

how do you love the man who lies
calls you baby when you pull all your hair out doesn't leave when your
face limps
& your name smears blue inside his mouth

how do you love the present when the past cracks & smiles blowing
scorched earth
you want to catch

& still there is a third man
a man over there waiting in the moments ahead
pulls you two feet in front of your body your body
he makes you forget the broken body with traces of sound still in his
skin & his mouth
slits a prayer & he looks at you like he hears you like he fucked you
before you even met
& it's too much for the heart the heart
Here, now, not over there, but here, now, can you feel it, in my chest,
the claws rip at bone, the feathers beat against the ribs. When the heart
cracks a bird crawls out.

Original poem by Kat Moore,
English PhD Student,
University of North Texas

Deleuze and Guattari Studies 12.4 (2018): 553
DOI: 10.3366/dlgs.2018.0331
© Kat Moore
www.euppublishing.com/dlgs

Bodies, *Gestus*, Becoming: Cinema as a Technology of Gender and (Post)memory

Belén Ciancio   National Scientific and Technical Research Council
(CONICET), Argentina

Abstract

The first issue this essay examines is the articulation of the cinema of
the body, the feminine *gestus*, and the 'political cinema', which begins
with the philosophical shout, 'Give me a body, then!' and ends with the
'Third World Cinema' as a cinema of memory. How is this Deleuzian
concept in tension with the one proposed here of 'missing body'? The
second issue concerns the importance of the body for theory and practice
within feminist film theory and queer theory. The question of the body is
introduced in-between these two lines in the context of a series of Latin
American documentaries. The final problem is then how to see and show
a body that is missing, like an outside of the body image, and of a certain
regime of the visible and the audible that tends to be fixed in topics by
the production of technologies of (post)memory.

Keywords: Cinema Studies, postmemory, feminism, body, gender,
Third World Cinema

I. Introduction

Different concepts of body persist in philosophical and film theory
essays, which coincide with some of the questions raised by Deleuze
concerning the filmed body, the filming body, the body of the spectator.
These concerns are often raised in relation to documentary (Comolli
2002), the digital body (Badiou 2004), and the hypnotised body

Deleuze and Guattari Studies 12.4 (2018): 555–571
DOI: 10.3366/dlgs.2018.0332
© Edinburgh University Press
www.euppublishing.com/dlgs

of the cinema (Bellour 2009). These film theories and philosophical essays present a hypothesis of the fascination of the 'cinematic body' that goes further than the semiotic/psychoanalytic model which was proposed initially by Christian Metz and given a feminist dimension by Laura Mulvey (Shaviro 1993). However, most of these theories and perspectives mentioned ponder a neutral body, not a gendered, sexuated, racialised or 'otherised' body, like the bodies in what Deleuze calls 'minor cinemas'. Thus, they do not include the question of the 'missing people', or the 'becoming people', indicative of Third World Cinemas (Deleuze 2000: 216–17). Moreover, they do not adequately address what is called here the 'missing body' which arises through the continuities and discontinuities of 'political cinema' and which, in *Cinema 2*, ends with the idea of the 'minor cinema' as a cinema of memory not linked with the past but with the future.

After studying the significance of these omissions, I consider the traditions of feminist film theory and queer theory, whereby the body (and embodiment) is one of the most important elements for theory and practice (see Mulvey 1975; de Lauretis 1987; Preciado 2009; Braidotti 2000). Some of these last theories present a different perspective than Deleuze's about women's cinema, and women in cinema, and some of them propose a critique of the Deleuzian concepts of woman and becoming woman (de Lauretis 1987). Similarly, some cinema scholars suggest a critique of the concept of minor cinema (Aguilar 2015).

In this context, one of the concepts that is in tension with becoming woman is 'technologies of gender', which offers even other dimensions when it is thought as 'technologies of memory', as I propose here. Teresa de Lauretis, one of the first authors to introduce the term *queer theory*,[1] argued that gender consists not of a sexual difference *per se*, but of a representation, and 'all of Western Art and high culture (and, of course, films and popular culture, too, we can say) is the engraving of the history of that construction' (de Lauretis 1987: 3). In this sense, women are unrepresentable except as representation. The concept of 'technologies of gender' allows us to think the question of the body in cinema not only in terms of the deconstruction or the undoing of gender or as a resistance to becoming woman, but in relation to the problem of what could be called 'technologies of memory'. This is a concept that follows one of the lines opened by Michel Foucault, which he defined as 'a complex political technology' (Foucault, qtd in de Lauretis 1987: 3) which is also linked with the concept of postmemory. This problem does not only concern the legitimacy and the (im)possibility of representing horror with images (see Didi-Huberman 2004); it also concerns other questions: how to do things with images, which implies performativity, and what gender, what body, what memory, and what 'people' are performed through images. In this context some of the film theories focused on Latin American cinemas that retake the concept of the 'becoming people', Third World Cinema or 'minor cinema' present some questions in common with the feminist critique of becoming woman (see Aguilar 2015).

It is necessary to think these questions, as well as the limits of Deleuzian concepts, in light of non-Western European societies such as Latin American and Indian,[2] not only because they both have strong cultural industries expanded in the field of cinema and television, but because, in the case of Latin America, some countries like Argentina and Guatemala have been involved in the search for justice concerning acts of genocide.[3] Meanwhile, the disappearance of forty-three students on 26 September 2014 from the Ayotzinapa Rural Teachers' College in Mexico, and the silence over migrants who have been lost crossing frontiers or at sea, shows that the 'disappearing power' referred to by Pilar Calveiro as a biopolitical tool used to erase subversion or quell unrest (Calveiro 1998) still functions in the present. The way this power functions is not unconnected with the way those events are shown in mass media.

Significantly, there has been a rebirth of the cinema in Argentina and in other Latin American countries in the past few years. In particular, those focused on the practice of documentary represent important lines of discontinuity with the previous militant and political cinema. A part of this production is focused on the recent past and is considered to produce what has been called postmemory, which is a kind of creative elaboration of the past in order to deal with trauma or reclaim a past that has been lost, co-opted, prosecuted or institutionalised, by political, juridical or social forces.[4] This essay tries to think how one of the most important questions in these recent films is not only the relation between generations or the (im)possibility of representing the past, but how to see and show a body that is missing – missing, like an outside of the body image of a certain regime of the visible and the audible, in the production of 'technologies of memory'. Moreover, these films, and other practices, like postporn,[5] become a new way of thinking the philosophical shout, 'Give me a body, then!' Thus, this work addresses how the question of the body and Deleuze's contention that the body 'forces to think' in a mutation of thought related to yet separated from the brain shares some assumptions with problematic concepts and experiences such as gender and memory. Both of them not only present an explicit social and political dimension but, going beyond Deleuzian cinema studies, deal with the problem of representation.

II. Body Cinema

'Give me a body, then!' sounds at first like another form of a legal petition historically linked to the demands of justice and memory, the 'habeas corpus'. But, according to Deleuze, the sentence states the formula of a philosophical reversal, or mutation, of a force that is not the one of thought but the one that thrusts thought into the categories of life and belief (not anchored in this or another world, or even in language, but in the body) – in this case, through cinema. The filmed body is claimed, at first and paradoxically, as a lost link with the world – a loss that especially concerns occidental philosophers.[6] This shout expresses a dualism that runs all through the history of philosophy and where the soul, the spirit, thought, and even the brain were denied to women, children, indigenous, non-occidentals – all of them considered just bodies. Now the philosopher shouts for a body, needs a body and a belief in it. This reversal of the relations between thought and body, expressed in the shout, 'Donnez-moi donc un corps!', is one of three mutations of the image of thought Deleuze identifies in his work on cinema.[7]

I consider that the chapter beginning with this formula (Deleuze 2000: ch. 8) is an intensely important one for several reasons: (1) the idea of a body cinema and a brain cinema – suggesting in some parts a dualism, even when the attitudes of the body that become the *gestus* are finally understood by Deleuze as the true categories of the spirit; (2) the introduction of the idea of a 'feminine *gestus*' in some films by and about women; (3) the question of a political cinema, in a trance,[8] and, with it, the idea of a missing people in European political post-war cinema and becoming in Third World Cinema; and finally (4) the move beyond classification of the movement-image and the time-image and also beyond a Bergsonian concept of memory.

When Deleuze refers to the body cinema, he goes beyond the sensorimotor schema that articulates the narration. He proposes the concept of Brechtian *gestus*, but not with the epic dimension that it has for Brecht, seeing the body attitudes for example in the *nouvelle vague* and the post-*nouvelle vague*. In a Nietzschean and Spinozist way, the body is no longer the obstacle that separates thought from itself. On the contrary, it 'is that which it plunges into or must plunge into, in order to reach the unthought, that is life' (Deleuze 2000: 189). With this statement, Deleuze reminds us of Artaud's first belief in the body and the flesh and, from there, of the relationship between cinema and theatre. He describes the attitudes concerning the everyday and ceremonial body in the films of Antonioni, Bene, and Cassavetes and in the experimental films of Warhol, as well as the passage of attitudes or postures to the *gestus*, a formal chain of attitudes, in the fiction films of Godard. Finally, Deleuze ends by expressing a certain weariness of the 'cinema of the bodies', and its repeated exaltation ceremonies, its cult of gratuitous violence, and what he calls 'the installation of a culture of catatonic and hysterical attitudes' (195).[9] In this part of his studies, Deleuze refers to the cinema of Chantal Akerman, Agnes Varda, and Michele Rosier with a perspective that differs from feminist film theory. He mentions a *feminine gestus*,[10] where bodies show a chain of states that remains open-ended: 'descending from the mother or going back to the mother, it serves as a revelation to men, who now talk about themselves' (196). Meanwhile, the woman's body achieves a strange nomadism, which makes it traverse ages, situations, and places. Nomadism is compared to a literature that is present in the last works of Deleuze, where he speaks of Virginia Woolf as displaying a female *gestus* that captures the history of mankind and the world crisis:

> Female authors, female directors, do not owe their importance to a militant feminism. What is more important is the way they have produced innovation in cinema of bodies, as if women had to conquer the source of their own attitudes and the temporality which corresponds to them as individuals or common *gestus*. (Deleuze 2000: 197)

Deleuze does not mention that this 'descending from the mother' or 'going back to the mother' supposes a way of creating distance from the way that femininity was embodied and placed generally, thinking not only in the way that feminine places like the kitchen in *Saute ma ville* (1968) are seen by Akerman but also in experimental video like *Semiotics of the Kitchen* (Martha Rosler, 1975). The *gestus* here were not the ones that were socially expected for women in a kitchen, a difference from *Jeanne Dielman* (Chantal Akerman, 1975). In other words, though Deleuze emphasises some elements of femininity here, the question of the becoming woman is not particularly present in these cinema studies. It starts to appear as a becoming when Deleuze talks about a minor cinema of a people to come (which is why memory has to do with the future) but following now Kafka and Klee. Moreover, Deleuze does not talk specifically in filmic terms but returns to the 'impossibility' of writing: 'the minority film-maker [like Pierre Perrault] finds himself in the impasse described by Kafka: the impossibility of not "writing", the impossibility of writing in the dominant language, the impossibility of writing differently' (Deleuze 2000: 217). So, a specifically feminist reading is difficult to derive from Deleuze's treatment of film alone, and when the issue of becoming is broached it seems that Deleuze has moved away from women authors/artists. Therefore, the potential of Deleuze's concepts for some feminist appropriation is curtailed and there is a lacuna, which feminist and gender theorists such as de Lauretis and Braidotti will note, and contest, specifically with regard to what concerns becoming woman.

III. Technologies of Gender and Memory

During the same years that Deleuze writes his cinema studies, some events having to do with issues of memory and gender align with the problems proposed in *Cinema 2*, which redefine not only the field of film theory but also the philosophical aesthetic of collective memory in the Southern Cone and of feminism. On the one hand, there was the premiere of the documentary by Claude Lanzmann, *Shoah* (1985), which, in the words of Simon Schrebnik: 'This ... this ... no one can describe it. No one can recreate what happened here. Impossible' (my translation), introduces the problem of the witness and the unrepresentable (see Didi-Huberman 2004). The problem of representation and recollection is the representation of the 'this' (*Das*) and its impossibility (*Unmöglich*). In this film there are no piles of bodies like in *Night and Fog* (Alain Resnais, 1955) – a cinema of brain, for Deleuze – to show the genocide, just the voices of the witnesses, the bystanders, the experts, and the Nazis themselves. At the same time in the Southern Cone, the return to democracy will produce a cinema that intends to show the horror of the preceding years.[11] The inclusion of the Argentinian experience through these filmic narratives may show that the 'memory cinema' of that moment was not the same as in the Third Cinema.

On the other hand, from the field of feminism, de Lauretis begins to resume the work of feminist film criticism of narrative cinema. De Lauretis, like Deleuze, departs from the semiotic debates and from authors like Christian Metz, Pier Paolo Pasolini, and Charles Peirce, but she introduces, through Foucault and Althusser, the concept of 'technology of gender'. De Lauretis reviews the Deleuzo-Guattarian concept of becoming woman and retakes the critique of cinema defined as an apparatus in which 'cinematic codes create a gaze, a world and an object, thereby producing an illusion cut to the measure of desire' (Mulvey, qtd in de Lauretis 1984: 59). This is a desire identified as (and reduced to) male desire. Thus, Mulvey proposes the destruction of narrative and visual pleasure as the foremost objective of women's cinema. For de Lauretis (1985), the question is, 'What formal, stylistic or thematic markers point to a female presence behind the camera?' This cannot be answered with a generalisation or universalisation, because to ask whether there is a feminine or female aesthetic is for de Lauretis, following Audre Lorde, to 'remain caught in the master's house' or to 'legitimate the hidden agenda of a culture' (Lorde, qtd in de Lauretis 1985: 158). Instead, in the kind of cinema such as Akerman's, there would be no feminine *gestus*, or not just a feminine *gestus* but two different logics: the one of the character and the other of the camera and the director, usually considered as the male point of view, a perspective that in the last few years, with a lot of women working in the field of cinema and audio-visual, should have changed, just as the concept of woman itself is changing. Cinema, in this perspective, has to do not only with women or with 'Woman'[12] but also with the construction of gender, as a social and political technology. There would be no female *gestus per se*, before any representation or performativity.[13] Instead, it would arise in its construction between the character, the camera/director, and the spectator. This is a difference with Deleuze's idea of the 'feminine *gestus*' and also with a dramatic Brechtian *gestus* that de Lauretis's intervention allows us to see.

Some years later, in *Technologies of Gender* (1987), de Lauretis will continue this reflection by regarding gender not only as sexual difference but also as a representation and as a construction. This has implications for the material life of individuals. This process occurs in a specific historical moment, not only through what is traditionally considered 'ideological state apparatuses', but also through the practices that resist them, such as feminism. Likewise, the construction of gender is also affected by its deconstruction: 'For gender, like the real, is not only the effect of representation but also its excess, what remains outside discourse as a potential trauma which can rupture or destabilize, if not contained: any representation' (de Lauretis 1987: 3). Through this idea of the outside as excess, de Lauretis implies that the construction of gender is both the product and the process of its representation.

In the same text, de Lauretis follows Braidotti's first analysis in which she discusses the forms that femininity assumes in the work of Deleuze, Foucault, Lyotard, and Derrida, and critiques the refusal by each philosopher to identify femininity with real women:

On the contrary, it is only by giving up the insistence on sexual specificity (gender) that women, in their eyes, would be the social group best qualified (because they are oppressed by sexuality) to foster a radically 'other' subject, de-centred and de-sexualized. (de Lauretis 1987: 24)

By displacing not only the ideology but also what she considers the reality and the historicity of gender into a diffuse, decentred, or deconstructed subject, these theories make an appeal to women, naming the process of such displacing with the term 'becoming woman'. For de Lauretis, this process denies sexual difference (and gender) as components of subjectivity in 'real women'. By denying the history of women's political oppression and resistance and the epistemological contribution of feminism to the redefinition of subjectivity and sociality, these philosophers see in women the privileged repository of 'the future of mankind'. This supposes the old mental habit of philosophers of 'thinking the masculine as synonymous with universal, the mental habit of translating women into metaphor' (Braidotti, qtd in de Lauretis 1987: 24). The point is that, like sexuality, gender is not a property of bodies or something originally existent in human beings, it is 'the set of effects produced in bodies, behaviors, and social relations' (de Lauretis 1987: 3), as the deployment of what Foucault called 'a complex political technology' (Foucault, qtd in de Lauretis 1987: 3). This set of effects is not abstract. They produce the 'real woman' that did not exist before, remembering de Beauvoir's motto: 'one is not born, but rather becomes, a woman' (de Beauvoir 1949: 13). This paradox is similar to some that emerge when memory is thought as a technology, because of the supposition that memory is not just a natural, psychological, or spiritual faculty, but also a product of a social and cultural mediation, a set of effects.

Understanding gender in this way eliminates the worry of metaphorising 'woman' because it is the real conditions (effects) that are being considered in order to reach a conclusion about the description of gender. These attempts to address the significance of Deleuze's work for and about women suggest that it is always problematic and depends on other concepts such as becoming, molar, molecular, and minor and how they are understood (or resisted). For example, the first one is not exactly understood by de Lauretis, but she sees other problems related to gender as concepts that are invisible for Deleuze; so, rather than referring to a medical or historical use of concepts, she is reinventing them, linking this with the radical feminist movement to produce a critical concept of gender, as she will do with 'queer'.[14]

But, some years after this critique, Braidotti affirms that Deleuze is a great help to feminists because he de-essentialises the body, sexuality, and sexed identities. Deleuze and Guattari provide different ways of understanding the body in its connections with other bodies (human and nonhuman, animate and inanimate), linking organs and biological processes to material objects and social practices. Yet, Braidotti also affirms that the Deleuzian body is ultimately an 'embodied memory': 'Neither a sacralised inner sanctum, nor a pure socially shaped entity, the enfleshed Deleuzean subject is rather an "in-between": it is a folding-in of external influences and a simultaneous unfolding outwards of affects' (2000: 159). Unlike her first critique of becoming woman (cited by de Lauretis), Braidotti thinks here the importance of the becoming as an active process but is also wary of the limits of the idea of the body as a pure representation, remembering a materiality but also its transformations in the contemporary figurations of the body, understood as 'abstract technological constructs fully immersed in advanced psycho-pharmacological industry, bio-science and the new media' (161). As a feminist of sexual difference whose work diverges from constructivist theories of gender and from essentialism, Braidotti thinks that in the middle of these apparently unlimited prosthetic promises of perfectibility and technoscience, Deleuze's philosophy lends precious help to those who remain 'proud to be flesh!' (161). But, beside this affirmation of Braidotti, it is necessary to remember that, even when Deleuze's concept of image is Bergsonian and the body as image is understood materially, bodies are always in a process of technological devices, and flesh is normalised in the mainstream industrial culture. In other words, the body is an object of standardisation and an idealisation that differs from the 'real woman', or from migrants who are considered *mere* bodies, thus 'not human', an experience that reflects the opposite of the philosophers who shout, 'Give me a body, then!'

In these contexts, audio-visual practices like postporn expect to produce a desubjugation, a new way of thinking the 'body cinema', the feminine *gestus*, and the technologies of gender. Not only because most of the producers of these works that often 'undo' the codes of the mainstream pornography are women, but because many times they put in crisis the effects of representation. This problematisation of the body and the subject/object of representation in postpornography,[15] which goes beyond Deleuze or departs from other conceptual universes and practices, has some points in common with postmemory. Therefore, both Braidotti and Preciado have introduced the question of the pharmacological and technological modifications of the body and affirm a link with Deleuze.

What I have tried to show here is the difference between the feminine *gestus* in Deleuze, and the concept of technologies of gender, as well as the changes in the position of Braidotti and that she was one of the first to introduce the question of the pharmaco-woman (attributed generally to Preciado). Finally, I introduce Preciado, because her idea of the *corpus pornograficus* provides an idea of all the opposite of the philosophical shout that demands a body. Though there is no room here to do a complete analysis of Preciado's hypothesis about the 'pharmaco-woman' produced with oestrogen, the idea of a 'biotechnological reality' where bodies are deprived of all civic context (migrants, deported, sex workers, laboratory animals) is important. These bodies become *corpora pornographica* whose lives lack any right to citizenship, authorship, and to work, composed by and subject to self-surveillance and global mediatisation (see Preciado 2013).

IV. Techno-membranes of Memory and Postmemory: The Becoming People, the Missing People, and the Missing Body

According to Deleuze, a people in the process of becoming could only appear in the film production of the Third World in which the people are present but shown in constant becoming. This way of addressing Third World Cinema, as a cinema of memory, implies a positive assessment of the 'state of permanent crisis' of collective identities in the periphery. A moment of crisis, or trance, is a moment of actualisation of memory because the circuit of perception diverges from the regular functioning of a sensorimotor schema, in which an action is followed by its corresponding reaction.

In the course of his writings, Deleuze's concept of memory shows a mutation. At first, it is identified with the Bergsonian idea of duration – contrasting human time with the time of Physics; the actual/virtual pair is understood in opposition to the real/possible pair. He asks not what memory is, whether real or fictional, but how it works: How is a virtual memory actualised in an experience here and now? Then, in his studies of film, Deleuze gives an almost spatial, biological, and social meaning to memory, casting it as a surface or membrane (following Simondon), a permeable boundary between the inside and outside, the collective and individual, and the private and public. Memory, in its social meaning, is a matter of minorities; here the private immediately becomes political. Minorities are identifiable because they do not seek to become the majority or to be hegemonic: instead, in their process of becoming each *self* names a people in terms of what that people lacks and what it could be (Deleuze 2000: 220–2).

For Deleuze, the Third World is always a cinema of memory. Because of this, it becomes a space for utopian projections and the promotion of collective statements. In *Cinema 2*, utopia finds a place in Third World Cinema, as the tension between the (im)possible and the virtual that goes beyond mere representation, allowing him to propose a future (of a people to come) that seems to have no past. This cinema is a kind of fabulation, the invention of a minor people.[16] In proposing fabulation, Deleuze goes beyond concepts of movement-image and time-image, giving it a futural and political dimension. It is possible, though, to question some of his assumptions. On the one hand, he does not take into account all of the dimensions of political film; in particular, he overlooks one of the most highly developed film practices at the time of his writing, the documentary of what is often called the Third Cinema. On the other hand, because he does not allude to the context of the Cold War or to the violent interruptions of Latin American filmmaking during the dictatorships, his analysis is incomplete, or produces the same projection with the Third World as did becoming woman (women as the privileged repository of the future of mankind). Finally, while labelling Third World Cinema as political film and a cinema of memory, a certain regionalisation of these questions is assumed: 'It is as if the whole memory of the world is set down on each oppressed people, and the whole memory of the I comes into play in an organic crisis. The arteries of the people to which I belong, or the people of my arteries' (Deleuze 1989: 221).

However, Deleuze's thoughts concerning the political possibilities related to minoritisation coincide with the perspectives of many filmmakers, especially documentary filmmakers, at the time. For example, from the perspective of liberation cinema, in films such as *The Hour of the Furnaces* (Octavio Getino and Fernando E. Solanas, 1966–8), filmmakers distinguished between the liberating concept of memory and the dominating concept of history (Getino 1984). The people in Glauber Rocha's *Entranced Earth* (1967) were in the streets during the most intense moments of the film, the same as the character who questions the political power, the poet and journalist Paulo Martins. *The Hour* ... begins with images of street protest and with the titles: 'our first gesture, our first word: LIBERATION'.[17]

Nevertheless, by the time Deleuze writes his studies, the trance film, which concerns the body in trance and becoming people, is not the same in Latin America. For instance, at the end of the 1960s, Rocha was preparing an 'epic-didactic' film, *América nuestra*, that he never completed which had a different narrative than *Entranced Land* (1967), which expected to return to a dialectic logic. In Brazil, for example, they were producing some of the most important documentaries about the recent past, like *João Goulart: Jango* (Silvio Tendler, 1984) and *Twenty Years Later* (Eduardo Coutinho, 1984). In Argentina, during the trial, sometimes called the Argentine Nuremberg, films such as *The Official Story* (Luis Puenzo, 1985), *The Night of the Pencils* (Hector Olivera, 1986), and *South* (Fernando Solanas, 1988) were produced, as were documentaries like *The Lost Republic I–II* (Miguel Perez, 1983) and *Juan, as if Nothing Had Happened* (Carlos Echeverría, 1987), or the experimental film *Habeas Corpus* (Jorge Acha, 1986). There was also, during the 1980s, the work of one of the most important feminist filmmakers, María Luisa Bemberg, with movies like *Camila* (1984), which was seen as an allegory of the dictatorship.

With different resources, such as the melodramatic elements in fiction, documentary research, or experimentation, some of these film and documentary-makers attempt to put the disappeared body or the act of disappearance 'in the scene'. They recall a missing body, not only in a collective sense or with an epic gesture, as in the first ending of the *The Hour* ... in which the most shocking image is the face of Che at the end, like a dead Jesus, but appealing for a revolution. 'They' refers to films like *Juan, as if Nothing Had Happened*, *Habeas Corpus*, *The Lost Republic*, and *The Night of the Pencils*. These reflect a different way of showing the people and the missing people. In the 1980s we see mostly the consequences of the repression, while in the Third Cinema of the 1960s and 1970s, the struggle. These films of the 1980s showed on the screen something that could not circulate in a speech or in the public sphere: disappearance (see Kriger 1994). The best known among those films appeared in educational spaces with a pedagogical purpose, until now. This is why it is possible to consider that moment and those films as the beginning of the construction of a 'technology of memory'.[18] In the 1970s, films like *The Hour* ..., and others of the Third Cinema, did not have a massive circulation, but one reserved to militants or political organisations as well as a certain masculine gaze. Meanwhile, films like *The Official Story* were considered films for women, and documentaries like *The Lost Republic* were shown in schools.

On the other hand, some of the documentaries of critical memory, produced in the last few decades – like *M* (Nicolas Prividera, 2007), *The Blondes* (Albertina Carri, 2003) *Papá Ivan* (María Inés Roqué, 2004), and *Finding Victor* (Natalia Bruchstein, 2004) – are embodied memories that expect to break with the flux of repeated topics, because they do not begin from 'general fact' or from 'collective memory' but from the difficulties of narrating the labyrinths of a singular memory with images and sounds. The first three evoke a missing body, at the same time as searching for a first-person statement. Those singular memories can also be called techno-membranes of memories, considering two dimensions: (1) a technology of memory and (2) a surface contact with its outside. They participate in a double becoming that involves, in some cases, becoming child. This idea of techno-membranes opposes a bifurcated idea of memory (something completely constructed or something essential or biological), showing rather the imbrication of materiality and socio-technological mediation.

One may ask then, which should be the *gestus* of/for the (re)presentation of a missing body? In order to answer this question, we must examine the particularities of these films. In *The Blondes*, there are no pictures of Roberto Carri and Ana María Caruso, Albertina's missing parents, and the limits of the representation are performed with Playmobil toys, while in Prividera's *M* there are lots of images of Marta Sierra, the missing mother. Yet the moment of the recollection about her kidnapping, during a testimony, is portrayed from a detuned TV, not the typical footage or archive photos that are usually seen in historical documentaries. Prividera, like in *Finding Victor*, also uses similar resources to *Archeology of Absence* (Lucila Quieto, 2002), which is a photographic exhibition that produces a *gestus* in which images have been pieced together through montages of old and new photos, even of the now adult children standing before images of their young parents, which creates an imagined or impossible present, anachronistically, given the content of the images. For example, there is an image of Marta Sierra and her son Nicolás; Nicolás was not present in the original picture, yet he is same age as Marta in this version of the photo. This is considered an impossible photo because it seems as if it is a 'real' photo with the mother, but it is impossible temporally because of the ages. Thus, with different narrative resources, those images evoke virtual bodies that are disappeared, by producing a *gestus*, not only with the photographic resource but also by bringing on stage the body of the author, a body in the act of searching (*M*) or a body performed by an actress (*The Blondes*), to produce more distancing effects.

Because of this use of photography or because of the affection and emotions that they involve, these films have been considered to be dealing with the construction of postmemories. But one of the principal problems of this interpretation is that it supposes a generation of descendants that were not there. These filmmakers, like other people of this generation whose testimonies appear in their documentaries, are themselves survivors. They grew up during the last dictatorship, except a few who were in exile, not after it.[19] Ultimately, postmemory supposes a cultural industry of memory that was not expanded in the Southern Cone until recent years, rather than the juridical dimension of the testimony that is present in a documentary like *M*. One could say that these works are not postmemories of the authors, but that they produce postmemories in a global spectator who can have access to these works through the web, in the sense of Hirsch's concept of 'connective memory' (Hirsch 2012). Finally, what these images have in common with postporn is that they put in question the usual representation or narratives about the last dictatorship. They have to do with the paradox of becoming subject of the narration, not the object and not just the victims, but the filmmakers, and, as such, they can be critiqued.

The production of technologies of memory on a global level continues today, mostly with new devices, social networks, and new museological, cultural, and academic productions. It is indispensable, then, especially for the construction of gender and memories, to find those images of the 'other side', of the 'out of the shot', or even the 'disappeared' of official discourses on memory and postmemory. Those images and *gestus* are more necessary when, recalling the opening phrase of George Steiner in *The Last Bolshevik* (Chris Marker, 1992), 'It is not the past that dominates us, but the images of the past.'

Notes

1. Paul B. Preciado has developed some of the questions raised by de Lauretis in a short history about the word 'queer' (2009).
2. A first version of this work was presented at the Third International Deleuze Studies in Asia Conference 2015. I do not pretend in this text to introduce a perspective about Hindi cinema, popular Indian cinema or about Bollywood. There are a lot of significant works in India and in the field of international film studies about this, with terms like 'masala-image' (see Martin-Jones 2011).
3. For instance, the trials in different Argentinian cities since 2005, and the trial against Efrain Rios Montt in Guatemala in 2013.
4. 'Postmemorial work ... strives to reactivate and reembody more distant social/national and archival/cultural memorial structures by reinvesting them with resonant individual and familial forms of mediation and aesthetic

expression' (Hirsch 2012: 33). My point is not to advocate 'for' postmemory (Amado, Aguilar) or 'against' it (Sarlo), but rather to show its operation and limits, in this case situated in Argentina (see Ciancio 2015). Some other related concepts are affiliative postmemories and connectives postmemories. These last two do not concern familiar or blood ties, but are produced by other ways: social networks, for example.

5. The first use of 'postporn' is attributed to Wink van Kempen (photographer) and then to Annie Sprinkle (ex-porn star). Today it refers to the becoming subject of the abject objects of pornographic representation: women, sexual minorities, non-white people, transsexuals, travesties, intersex, transgender. The works of Nadia Granados (Colombia), Diana Torres (Spain), Leo Silvestri (Argentina) and Maria Llopis (Barcelona) are considered postporn.

6. 'It's quite curious that a thinker (Kierkegaard) utters this shout – this is a philosophical shout: "Give me a body, then!" Because for long periods thinkers, they rather pretended that ... they do not have too much body' (Deleuze 1984: 189; my translation).

7. The first one is the substitution of belief for knowledge; the second, the substitution of a *Dehors* (Outside) for an 'inside'.

8. The concept of trance is from the film *Entranced Earth* (Glauber Rocha, 1967), and the interpretation of tropicalism is from the Brazilian intellectual Roberto Schwarz.

9. The relationship between hysteria, cinema and visual arts is not only a question of the *nouvelle vague*. It is present in the hypothesis of the 'invention' of a visual device, the device 'hysteria' in *La Salpêtrière* (see Didi-Huberman 2014).

10. This concept comes from Brecht and the interpretation of it by Barthes in *Mother Courage* (1941), considering the *gestus* not as a ceremony, but rather a ceremonialising of the most current, banal attitudes (see Deleuze 2000). The difference from the first Brechtian theory is that this *gestus* is not immersed in an epic drama.

11. Meanwhile, in Buenos Aires the *Trial of the Juntas* (1985) was produced, and for the first time an Argentinian film, *The Official Story* (Luis Puenzo, 1985), won an Oscar. These events are not present in Deleuzian cinema studies; his idea of a cinema of memory is focused on the films of the 'Third World', specifically on the films of Rocha.

12. For de Lauretis, *Born in Flames* (Lizzie Borden, 1983) showed that this concept of Woman produces an invisibility about representations of class, race, language and social relations. See de Lauretis 1985: 168.

13. De Lauretis does not use the Butlerian concept of performativity, but her concept of 'technologies of gender' has points in common with Butler. For a reading of performativity and technologies of gender as a subjectification in decolonial feminism, see Espinosa-Miñoso 2003.

14. This question is also problematic in the way that Deleuze understands homosexuality, transsexuality, and intersexuality, because it is not the conventional meaning, it is a philosophical question. For Preciado, 'becoming woman' and 'molecular homosexuality' are related; the latter concept makes a series of demands on Deleuze, similar to the critiques of de Lauretis and Braidotti (see Preciado 2002).

15. The relation between certain pornography and the representation of horror, the shot of sexual humiliation, is also present in the theory of postmemory (see Hirsch 2012) and in the written work of Nicolás Prividera (see Prividera 2014).

16. Some authors critique this idea of minoritisation because of its ethnocentrism (Aguilar 2015).

17. The capitalisation is in the original, repeated seven times.

18. This would be a different social function from the Third Cinema of the 1960s and 70s, which produced a memory that went back to the Spanish conquest to show the colonial condition.
19. Some of them were born in concentrations camps. See the testimonies in other documentaries considered postmemories: *(h) Stories of Everyday Life* (Andrés Habegger, 2001) and in *Grandchildren (Identity and Memory)* (Benjamín Ávila, 2004).

References

Aguilar, Gonzalo (2015) *Más allá del pueblo: Imágenes, indicios y políticas del cine*, Buenos Aires: Fondo de Cultura Económica.
Badiou, Alain (2004) 'El cine como experimentación filosófica', in Gerardo Yoel (ed.), *Pensar el cine 1*, Buenos Aires: Manantial, pp. 23–81.
Bellour, Raymond (2009) *Le Corps du cinema: Hypnoses, émotions, animalités*, Paris: P.O.L.
Braidotti, Rosi (2000) 'Teratologies', in Ian Buchanan and Claire Colebrook (eds), *Deleuze and Feminist Theory*, Edinburgh: Edinburgh University Press, pp. 156–72.
Calveiro, Pilar (1998) *Poder y desaparición: Los campos de concentración en la Argentina*, Buenos Aires: Colihue.
Ciancio, Belén (2015) '¿Cómo (no) hacer cosas con imágenes? Sobre el concepto de posmemoria', *Constelaciones: Revista de Teoría Crítica*, 7, pp. 503–15.
Comolli, Jean-Louis (2002) 'L'Anti-spectateur, sur quatre films mutants', *Images documentaires*, 44, pp. 9–40.
de Beauvoir, Simone (1949) *Le Deuxième Sexe*, Paris: Gallimard.
de Lauretis, Teresa (1984) *Alice Doesn't: Feminism, Semiotics, Cinema*, Bloomington: Indiana University Press.
de Lauretis, Teresa (1985) 'Aesthetic and Feminist Theory: Rethinking Women's Cinema', *New German Critique*, 34, pp. 154–75.
de Lauretis, Teresa (1987) *Technologies of Gender: Essays on Theory, Film and Fiction*, Bloomington: Indiana University Press.
Deleuze, Gilles (1984) *Cinéma/pensée cours 68 du 06/11/1984–2*, available at < http://www2.univ-paris8.fr/deleuze/article.php3?id_article=366 > (accessed 10 December 2015).
Deleuze, Gilles (1989) *Cinema 2: The Time-Image*, trans. Hugh Tomlinson and Robert Galeta, London: Athlone Press.
Didi-Huberman, Georges (2004) *Images malgré tout*, Paris: Minuit.
Didi-Huberman, Georges (2014) *Invention de l'hystérie: Charcot et l'iconographie photographique de la Salpêtrière*, Paris: Macula.
Espinosa-Miñoso, Yuderkys (2003) 'A una década de la performatividad: de presunciones erróneas y malos entendidos', *Otras Miradas*, 3:1, pp. 27–44.
Getino, Octavio (1984) 'Memoria popular y cine', in *Notas sobre cine argentino y latinoamericano*, Mexico: Edimedios, pp. 97–110.
Hirsch, Marianne (2012) *The Generation of Postmemory: Writing and Visual Culture after the Holocaust*, New York: Columbia University Press.
Kriger, Clara (1994) 'La revisión del proceso militar en el cine de la democracia', in Claudio España (ed.), *Cine argentino en democracia: 1983/1993*, Buenos Aires: Fondo Nacional de las Artes, pp. 54–67.
Martin-Jones, David (2011) *Deleuze and World Cinemas*, London: Continuum.
Mulvey, Laura (1975) 'Visual Pleasure and Narrative Cinema', *Screen*, 16:3, pp. 6–18.

Preciado, Beatriz (2002) *Manifiesto contrasexual*, Barcelona: Anagrama.

Preciado, Beatriz (2009) 'Queer: Historia de una palabra', *Parole de queer*, 1, pp. 14–17.

Preciado, Beatriz (2013) *Testo Junkie: Sex, Drugs, and Biopolitics in the Pharmacopornographic Era*, New York: Feminist Press.

Prividera, Nicolás (2014) *El país del cine. Para una historia política del Nuevo Cine Argentino*, Córdoba: Los Ríos.

Shaviro, Steven (1993) *The Cinematic Body*, Minneapolis: University of Minnesota Press.

On Arbormosis: Becoming-Cyborg, Machinic Subjection, and the Ethico-Aesthetic of User-Friendly Design

S. L. Revoy   Queen's University

Abstract

This paper suggests that the imbrication of user-friendly software and the posthuman has increasingly been revealed as an intrinsically arborescent relationship, one premised upon the striation of personal information through different forms of software media and allowing for unprecedented avenues of control and subjective manipulation. My analysis begins with a conceptualisation of user-friendliness, tracing its development as the majoritarian style of software design. In assessing the effects of this process of subjective imbrication with arborescent software technology, it is suggested that one effect of the pathological asignification of instrumentality in the representation of software is the genesis of a topological space which allows for a capacity for control over the subjective becoming of others through control over digitally mediated perception. To illustrate this point, the revelations concerning Cambridge Analytica's use of targeted advertisements on Facebook to affect voting preferences during the 2016 American presidential election are examined as an example of the quotidian domination which is characteristic of the subjective condition of arbormosis. This analysis can be applied to issues of gender, technology, and modes of subjective control.

Keywords: Cambridge Analytica, dataveillance, control society, arborescence, Facebook, software studies

Deleuze and Guattari Studies 12.4 (2018): 572–593
DOI: 10.3366/dlgs.2018.0333
© Edinburgh University Press
www.euppublishing.com/dlgs

Importantly, the 'choices' operating systems offer limit the visible and the invisible, the imaginable and the unimaginable. You are not, however, aware of software's constant constriction and interpellation (also known as its 'user-friendliness'), unless you find yourself frustrated with its defaults (which are remarkably referred to as your preferences) . . .

(Wendy Chun, *Programmed Visions*)

Indeed, it may be that what is *unanticipated* about the injurious speech act is what constitutes its injury, the sense of putting its addressee out of control. The capacity to circumscribe the situation of the speech act is jeopardized at the moment of injurious address. To be addressed injuriously is not only to be open to an unknown future, but not to know the time and place of injury, and to suffer the disorientation of one's situation as the effect of such speech.

(Judith Butler, *Excitable Speech*)

The signifying possible and the seemingly arborescent possible are thus definitively imposed to the detriment of all rhizomatic possibilization.

(Félix Guattari, *The Machinic Unconscious*)

I. On Schizoanalysis and Feminist Theory

The alliance of Deleuze and Guattari's philosophy and feminism is a powerful, urgently needed conjunction of two theoretical projects invested in the interrogation of problematics arising from the oppressively arborescent organisation and representation of the human world. Feminist theory continues to expansively and innovatively critique the politics of oppression which are traditionally based in the violent demarcation of difference, especially defined through terms of sex, race, sexual orientation, gender, and class. Deleuze and Guattari's work serves to augment this project, one which is already deeply rhizomatic by necessity; indeed, feminism must constantly confront and theorise new intersectional configurations of desire which actualise the enduring politics of oppression, a politics which consistently generates innovative new assemblages which enable and embolden the cancerous lineage of violence which each new instance inevitably draws upon. In line with these needs, Deleuze and Guattari offer a unique conceptual methodology for feminist critique which 'allows us to better grasp our own assemblages of enunciation [and] the assemblages of enunciation to which we are adjacent' (Guattari 2009a: 205). Deleuze and Guattari's schizoanalytic methodology apprehends the world as interlocked by flows of desire, a dynamic force of attraction and repulsion which in its transcendental character exceeds the concrete or even experiential as a fundament of physical and metaphysical organisation. The concrete organisation of assemblages allows for both the appearance and rupture of stability. Thus, understanding schizoanalysis as a 'discipline for reading other modelling systems' (Guattari 2013: 18) unearths new opportunities to examine oppression as a stratum which is dispersed transversally throughout human organisation, practices, and technologies. This dispersal occurs in an especially intense and extensive form through the emergence of what Guattari (2013: 6) calls 'planetary computerization', an epochal shift in subjectivity towards cybernetically governed forms of machinic subjection. I am humbled to be able to make a small contribution to this excellent collective effort to foster the alliance of feminism and Deleuze and Guattari's philosophy by offering the first salvo in an ongoing critique of the negative ethico-aesthetic of user-friendly software design and its archly arborescent effects on the production of subjectivity.

The growing impingement of mass media upon the production of subjectivity greatly concerns the later Guattari, who conceptualises these components of subjectivity as an especially advanced type of capitalist technology capable of:

> bear[ing] down on the basic functioning of the perceptive, sensorial, affective, cognitive, linguistic, etc. behaviors grafted to capitalist machinery ... Alienation by means of images and ideas is only an aspect of a general system of enslavement of their fundamental modes of semiotization, both individual and collective. (Guattari 2009c: 262)

An important purpose of these technologies of semiocapitalism[1] is the continuous representation of structural powers of oppression as normal and valorised. If 'power is the resuscitation of meaning' (Massumi 1992: 20) then the seizure of sensory meaning-making via mass media constitutes a new threshold of power for the enactment of oppression as a normative aesthetic condition. In this later work, Guattari expresses a deep concern with the perceptual investment already demanded of such media as television (1995: 16–17), an especially interesting concern when contextualised as being first made in the burgeoning era of 24-hour news, a type of television which creates an engine for the constant interpretation and representation of events as a hyperreality unto itself. Guattari also writes in a pessimistically prescient fashion about the future of these technologies as modes of subjection which could invest into the subject a certain perceptual worldview, understanding mass media as an invasive ecological paradigm which contains extensifying and intensifying capacities to '[take] over the relaying of the production of values and of "normalising" icons in social libido' and to create a state of affairs wherein 'opinion and collective taste ... will be worked over by statistical apparatuses and apparatuses for modelling' (2015: 48, 11). This influence over human perception by semiocapitalistic desiring-machines, represented most concretely today through user-friendly software, has grown exponentially in the era of ubiquitous computing. It is therefore crucial to examine the values informing the production of such representations, especially as they serve to mediate and reflect different sorts of vitalistic experience[2] according to a carefully constructed aesthetic which is equally concerned with the signification and asignification of computational instrumentality. These politics of (a)signification are especially urgent as we become increasingly aware of the powerful ways in which such software and its logics have been used as a strategy for the multivalent exploitation, oppression, and control of the subject in cyberspace. This paper represents a preliminary effort to theorise the conditions of arbormosis and its connection to the explosion of cybernetic technologies, with a special focus on beginning to unpack the composite of rationalisms which inform the aesthetic values, or style, of contemporary software.

Understanding these values is especially important to feminist critique when considering the burgeoning subjective condition of becoming-cyborg and its relation to Haraway's (2016: 28–31) famous warnings against the potential 'informatics of domination' which might entrench and embolden the patriarchal organisation of society through the abuse of human–computer interaction. This question concerning the negotiation of domination as a pitfall of technological extension seems increasingly pertinent in such a deeply asymmetrical digital world where humanity's subjective imbrication with its digital environs is so extensive that it becomes necessary to ask, 'how do we maintain the distinction between the body itself and information about that body, if the body itself, in a way, now consists of information?' (van der Ploeg 2012: 180). The de-materialisation of the body as information, a process perhaps experienced most viscerally in quotidian life through social media, suggests the need for a new ethico-aesthetic theory for the oppressive metastabilisation of the posthuman subject in informational media, as a series of unpredictable cybernetic flows which are primarily captured, arrested for capitalisation or otherwise exploited, in structures such as profiles and databases while being ultimately represented as a narrowly filtered and idealised form of feedback to the subject in which instrumentality is left asignified and only the instantaneous results of the user's commands are visible.

The ever-shifting episteme of the body is an essential terrain of machinic subjection as such, and its discursive and practical realignment may allow that 'at different historical moments, out of the pressure of cultural, social, and material change new images and associations emerge' (Bordo 1993: 4). We see intense subjective pressure upon the body through the saturation of digital media and the politics its particular semiocapitalistic design brings to the (dis)embodiment and production of cyborg subjectivities. In light of these concerns, I will begin to conceptualise this aesthetic pressure on the cyborg facets of posthuman subjectivity as a product of 'user-friendliness', the majoritarian ethico-aesthetic of contemporary digital interface design which has gradually developed as an ideal apparatus of capture for both the deterritorialisation of the subject as information and the concurrent reterritorialising striations of a subject's digital self within rigid grammatical forms, from database to profile structures, all of which help reify a universal subjective mould that is often reflective of an implicit assumption of a privileged majoritarian subjectivity; this assumption is borne out particularly in the lack of privacy and protection from abuse that is common to many social media platforms. For the majority who are not majoritarian subjects, there is an extreme discord between the universal signification of the profile form as a site of interconnected utopian social expression and the experiences of oppression and abuse which often occur as the politics of difference violently manifest in digital spaces. Some of the most violent and abusive example of this disjunct have resulted when gender is at play.

I hope here to contribute to the ongoing critical enterprise of unpacking the philosophical and political calculus of digital interface design practices, by formulating its majoritarian style as a discursive problematic of rationality which has been used forcefully to remediate the world within a stratum of cybernetic organisation, a process dedicated to the purely arborescent recombination of reality and subjectivity within the digital. I refer to this process as arbormosis, in contrast to Guattari's hopeful – yet unfulfilled – prospective ethico-aesthetic of chaosmosis. I am particularly concerned here with the conception of user-friendly software design as a discursive unity, which effects a disempowering and exploitative representational form for the 'diagrammatic rhizome which tends to cover the mecanosphere globally' (Guattari 1995: 42) by creating a common faciality for personal computer technology which functions as a semiotic system of 'universal resonators' (Guattari 2011: 79) used to decode desire into the quantum flow of capitalism's libidinal economy in the most efficient manner possible, in this case as digital information.

User-friendly design is the result of ongoing processes of desiring-production, which involve the reification of grammatical structures for the capture of subjectivity, and the world as such, as data capital through the vector of arbormosis, the processual remediation of the world through digital tree-logic. The aesthetic rationality of user-friendly design transversally inflects the design of all contemporary commercial computer software, regardless of purpose, and critiquing its ideology reveals a complex of contradictory logics which have produced a situation entirely asignifying the molecular politics of software, producing instead a darkly rhizomatic black box of unethical human and machinic behaviour, a planetary structure for cybernetic control which always operates contra the placid molar imagery of standardised efficiency and empowerment signified by 'user-friendly' software.

While Guattari distinguishes between scientific and ethico-aesthetic paradigms in his proposals for a chaosmosis, it remains the unfortunate truth that even the most rationalistic, abstract, arborescent, and unified scientific paradigms may gather a compelling aesthetic force[3] by which to be organised and actualised as an ecological predicate of subjectivation in the fundamentally chaotic world, thus being established as a seductive and artificial redoubt, an episteme with a clearly defined regime of signs for the microfascistic[4] organisation of selfhood and society. This is the predicament which we see reflected in the unparalleled success of user-friendly design as the aesthetic of personal computing software, a cybernetic aesthetic of control characteristic not of chaosmosis but of arbormosis. User-friendly softwares and their processes of arbormosis are essential to understanding the current political situation of what Braidotti terms the 'mutual interdependence of bodies and technologies' (2006: 37) whose subjective condition it is the 'historical imperative' (99) of critical theory to attempt to apprehend. If cyborgs 'are the subject of our prosthetic culture in a complex web of dynamics and technologically mediated social relation' (37), then user-friendliness is the aesthetic of its faciality and the interfacial relation of humans to computers. Considering the very conditions of possibility for the production of cyborg subjectivity, if 'the possibility of the "I," of speaking and knowing the "I," resides in a perspective that dislocates the first-person perspective it conditions' (Butler 2005: 28) then the values of user-friendly aesthetics bear special scrutiny in the age of posthumanism, not least because of its apparent tendency to reify, stabilise, and intensify the capacity for traditional forms of oppression and exploitation, as well as fostering newly empowered modes for its electronic expression. This is especially effective due to the central place of user-friendly software in the subjective mould of becoming-cyborg through which human subjectivity increasingly is modulated in all its contexts and experiences.

The user-friendly bind therefore consists of three strands. First, a mediatory striation of lived affairs and the production of subjectivity according to grammatical forms of semiocapitalistic deterritorialisation. This striation simultaneously actualises universal conditions of subjecting domination through the implementation of standard forms of identity. This logic valorises the drive towards interconnection and pervasive mass sousveillance operating in a schizoid pattern according to algorithmic sortation and the capitalistically channelled surveillant desire of subjects within social media networks, ultimately with the interest in cultivating the sharing of more information to be evaluated and capitalised.

Second, the asignification of the instrumental force of software, creating an unrepresented political space with the capacity for novel forms of exploitation, oppression, and violence through control over the data and infrastructure of the mechanosphere. This rhizome of instrumental politics occurs as the asignified semiotic remainder of user-friendly design and its desire to represent software and cyberspace as stable and effective, a largely unchanging extension of user will. Resultantly, the politics of software functionality and its deterritorialisation of information and reterritorialisation of data is rendered consistently imperceptible in the experience of software as such.

Third, the insistent enunciation of user-friendliness as one of optimal, rational, simplistic efficiency in software design, a historically entrenched tradition and empirically validated discourse of best practices within software engineering that broadly emphasises the centralisation of control and asignification of instrumentality in the deployment of human–computer interfaces.

II. Rationalities of a User-Friendly Universe

Guattari furnishes a conceptual exemplar for a genealogical sketch of the formation of user-friendly design as it emerges from the earliest intellectual work on cybernetics and computer design, as well as the highly successful efforts of the State apparatus to overcode that work in service of bureaucratic capitalism. In his constellation of 'Universes of value' which diagram the genesis and failure of the Concorde commercial jet as a politically constituted entity, Guattari notes:

> – a diagrammatic Universe with plans of theoretical 'feasibility';
> – technological Universes transposing this 'feasibility' into material terms;
> – industrial Universes capable of effectively producing it;
> – collective imaginary Universes corresponding to a desire to make it see the light of day;
> – political and economic Universes leading, amongst other things, to the release of credit for its construction. (Guattari 1995: 48)

Many of the similarly differentiated Universes which stabilise and promote user-friendliness, 'install[ing] themselves at this machinic interface between the necessary actual and possibilist virtual' (Guattari 1995: 55), are likewise not products of software aesthetics or cybernetics as such, but of the capture of cybernetics within the circuits of bureaucratic capitalism and a broader regime of signs that is congruent with its axiomatic system of capitalistic desiring-production. Formal user-friendly design, as espoused by commercial personal computing designers like Brenda Laurel and Donald Norman,[5] coordinates four lines of arborescent rationality, lines which occasionally segment and frequently break down throughout the history of software design but which persist and cumulatively contribute molarised qualities or values which form a rigid 'linear discursivity' (48) consistently dominating the imaginary of user-friendly software as a regime of signs, and an ethico-aesthetic which presupposes the regime.

This structuring and control of digital information, an activity which characterises the arborescent lineage and essential pursuit of cybernetics (Pias 2016), emerges palpably as a new discursive unity shortly after the end of the Second World War (see Golumbia 2009: 83–93; Pickering 1995), and each existential territory of user-friendliness which has formed an effective discursive positivity regarding the aesthetic production of information has influenced the contemporary user-friendly style of software and its near-total asignification of computational politics.[6] The effectiveness or durability of these territories has often been commensurate with the sway of their encapsulating Universes of value, which 'constitute incorporeal enunciators of abstract machinic complexions compossible with discursive realities' (Guattari 1995: 55) informing the concrete practices which ultimately metastabilise the normative representation of information by proffering fully automatic user-friendly mimesis and its consequent asignification of instrumentality. The formal user-friendly approach, instituted and popularised through pedagogy and made commercially dominant by corporations such as Apple and Microsoft, represents a discursive formalisation and a planetary enunciation of an ethico-aesthetic for software which harmonises the complex balance sheet of desiring-machines operating upon the discourse of effective computer design, as cyberneticists, related intellectuals, and economic actors often offer competing and divergent views of the ideal representation of software. Indeed, there have been several 'rational' conceptions of information aesthetics which have altered the genealogical vector of the representation of information towards an increasingly automated and instrumentally asignified user-friendly style. These rationalities, the groups of statements which sediment in order to allow for the positing of the discourse of user-friendly design, are:

- Cybernetic rationalism, a set of presumptions underwriting the conceit of a science for the control of systems which conceives of the planet as comprised of interlocking looped systems which operate based upon feedback, for example a human sensing their surroundings and adapting to newly perceived threat information as a processual loop of sense – feedback – adaptation – sense, which constitutes a general method for comprehending and potentially manipulating these systems.
- Binary rationalism, a set of presumptions underwriting the praxis of representing information in a structural and stratified manner as data.[7] This rationalisation of information as data begins with the denotation of binary as the base of computational communication and the mathematical substrate of all matter.
- Bureaucratic rationalism, the overcoding ethico-aesthetic of the State apparatus.[8] This entrenched rationality effectively captures the aesthetic trajectory of cybernetics, reterritorialising the early logics of cybernetics within the desiring-machines of bureaucratic organisation and thusly producing a nascent form, certainly the logical bedrock, of user-friendly software design as a multifaceted strategy of control, capably extending the general capacity of bureaucratic organisations to increase their productivity and further arborise their subjects through the deployment of software.
- State rationalism, a planetary macropolitical strategy which incorporates cybernetics as a means for establishing new thresholds of power over citizens through the capture of data, occurring in conjunction with what Deleuze and Guattari refer to as the

State apparatus and especially the capitalist axiomatic, orienting the production and use of software towards being a medium for commodification and market exchange.

Cybernetic rationalism is a phenomenally successful conception of the world as arborised, composed of interlocked systems based upon feedback and an immanent desire for homeostasis, constituting a general model of activity occurring with absolute consistency down to the level of neuronal activity and therefore logically subject to arborescent management techniques generated through cybernetic experimentation (Wiener 1948: 4–29; 1950: 15–27). This rationalism originates in tandem, perhaps even in symbiosis, with the 'binary rationalism' emblemised by Shannon's information theory, a theory which helped normalise the purely informational nature of communication in binary terms of 0s and 1s and signal versus noise (Hayles 1999) while declaring semantics or affect secondary for the purposes of mathematically modelling information. This approach emphasises that the optimisation of communication, irrespective of content, is the primary concern of information science (Shannon 2016). For our purposes here, the nuances of binary and its gradual abstraction as naturalistically linguistic, later visually syntaxed, software interfaces are less important than the arborescent principle of stratification and asignification informing the early work of cyberneticists and information theorists like Claude Shannon and Norbert Wiener, who parsed the totality of communication and rooted out messier issues such as semantic context to suggest a universal method for the mathematical communication of information in what is the original moment of user-friendly design. As Katherine Hayles (1999: 50–4) has carefully argued, this is unproblematic as a method for creating a more efficient data signal, but deeply problematic when adopted as the cultural condition or popular perception of what she terms 'virtuality', wherein information is considered as entirely disembodied and immaterial; this perception is further viewed in culture as a natural and desirable outcome of technological efficiency. This view of information postulates a simulational stratum (information) for the planet which can be mathematically modelled and controlled. Again, while this may be unproblematic as a scientific enterprise, the broader political concerns eventually dominating the design, deployment, and use of computers and cybernetics have appropriated this logic and its technologies as a means to remediate the world in an image of oppressive capitalistic control.

III. Social Media, Schizoveillance, and Semiocapitalism

The contemporary phenomenon of social media, especially its most popular exponent, Facebook, serves as an excellent example of the composite of rationalisms resulting in formal user-friendly software design being used to remediate vitalistic experience within a domain of cybernetic control, thus allowing for its capture as data capital. Social media also provides one of the clearest examples of arbormosis at work as a process for the wholesale arborification of subjectivity in the image of digitised data capital, not just as a discourse or apparatus but as a conjunction of an ethical worldview, one in accordance with integrated world capitalism, with an aesthetic practice which reifies these ethics. The axiomatic territoriality of integrated world capitalism has found its greatest purchase thus far with its fervent adoption of cybernetic technologies, which today allow for the compelling simulation of essential aspects of life, such as social media, through a medium predicated upon absolutely quantifiable observation and control.

The total asignification of instrumental activity, as well as the overwhelming signifying field of metaphoric analogue imagery composing the experience of user-friendly software, creates an exploitative space for the arborising of the rhizomatic subjective condition it otherwise foments by using both the deployment of particular metaphoric signs and the information they deterritorialise as leverage to accelerate traditional forms of exploitation and violence against minoritarian subjects. This imagery, and the ethico-aesthetic which guides its deployment, serves to exercise its own form of oppressive control over the procession of digital imagery which constitutes the experience of a computer and the terms of perception for any subjective vector of becoming-cyborg, reserving captured information in a proprietary, asignified stratum of databases and administrative software. It is this extensive control over the deterritorialised data doubles of Facebook users which allowed them to be sold as informational capital to the firm Cambridge Analytica, which used Facebook's intensely intimate knowledge to target particular voting districts during the American presidential election campaign of 2016.[9] The litany of abhorrent abuses of power here is manifold, but perhaps most shocking is the careful manipulation of racial identity and the fraught state of racial politics in the United States to the advantage, of all people, of then-candidate Donald Trump. Special advertisements were designed specifically for voters who were not only identified through their Facebook data as racialised but whose Facebook data was used to form a psychological profile through which certain inferences could theoretically be made about political values and voting intentions through Big Data analysis. The combination of personal data purposefully categorised by Cambridge Analytica as minoritarian and their attendant capacity to psychometrically profile these voters allowed them to create curated anti-Clinton advertisements designed to appeal to anti-racist sympathies and other specific political values, though these attack ads obviously elided the egregious history of Trump's racial politics. So curated were these ads that, outside of the Facebook profiles originating in narrow geographic areas which contained both a slim margin of voting intention for Hillary Clinton and a complementary, psychometrically profiled set of voters to attempt to manipulate, much of the United States never saw these ads in their own Facebook feeds.

Clinton has indeed had historical issues in some of her public positions as they relate to racialised minorities and their structural persecution by the criminal justice system in the United States; the point here is not to adjudicate the relative merits of Clinton, but to suggest that this strategy by Cambridge Analytica is an incredible example of the functional power of semiocapitalism in a world saturated not only in mass media devices, but ones designed according to the asignified instrumental politics of user-friendly design. When this aesthetic is applied to the perception of social reality, including such crucial events as democratic elections, as well as the production of subjectivity writ large – a conjunction we see vividly in the success of websites such as Facebook – we can also see how this mediatory manipulation of reality emerges as a potential crisis of democracy and subjectivity as such which threatens the very capacity for informed consensus, divided as our senses are by hyperindividuated, algorithmically prefabricated images of the world, our fellow citizens, our political leadership, even the world of events and the interpretation of reality as such, a point Guattari rightly noted in his critique of television. With Cambridge Analytica, we see the political manipulation of minorities emerge with a new digital fervour aiming to compromise their experience of political reality through targeted manipulation which coordinates intense biopolitical and semiocapitalistic power to not only affect their perception but to attempt to profoundly and rapidly affect their subjective views on electoral politics sufficiently to control their exercise of the democratic franchise, either by dissuading votes for Clinton or converting voters to Trump.

The Cambridge Analytica case is horrifying but instructive in the facts of using user-friendly software like Facebook; experiencing social media subjectively means inevitably being subjected to feedback derived from dividuated subjectivities captured by Facebook or its clients, all of which are asignified yet constantly parsed as a ceaselessly productive component of one's own interactive relation with the site and of their own experience of becoming-cyborg, demonstrating in real time what Mark Poster correctly diagnosed in his comment that 'what typifies advanced society is not so much the opposite of justice, truth and compassion, but language situations which operate at a different register from that of co-present, contextual self-monitoring talk or the ideal speech situation' (1990: 80). This excellent point which contextualises his recapitulation of Foucault within the digital is described in his conception of the 'superpanoptic' function of databases:

> The structure or grammar of the database creates relationships among pieces of information that do not exist in those relationships outside of the database. In this sense databases constitute individuals by manipulating relationships between bits of information ... The discourse/practice of the Panopticon was a condition for a new form of biopower, a means of controlling masses of people for the development of industrial processes. Similarly, the discourse of databases, the Superpanopticon, is a means of controlling masses in the postmodern, postindustrial mode of information. (Poster 1990: 96)

The reterritorialisation of deterritorialised subjective data exerts superpanoptic force both by creating new relations of subjective knowledge through the extraction of information as data from user activity, and by reconstituting it in databased form as a surveillance or control commodity ready to be used to either intensify the deterritorialisation through the eliciting of further information or, as in Cambridge Analytica, apply control over the data double and knowledge of its contents to affect subjectivation and consequently mould the dividuated subject towards an unknowable array of exploitative ends, from shopping to vote manipulation.

While Poster's superpanoptic describes the linear intensification of surveillant power introduced by computers, we add that the superpanoptic is different, beyond just intensification, in that its uniquely asignified politics and networking of most computers creates a new architectural enunciation of control, a discursive condition of the posthuman subject which is sustained as a schizoid production of subjectivity as multiple mobile centres of power compete to know and affect user subjectivities, for reasons as varied as antisocial revenge, theft, and fraud, or consumer profiling in hopes of turning a national election, all gridded within the syntactical configurations of the user-friendly Internet, generated through the axioms of user-friendliness and its best practices. This generates an emergent type of cyborg group subjectivity organised around a single individual, generated by multiple lines of subjectivation upon the individual subject by a schizoid array of surveillant desiring-machines, drawing upon and occasionally reflecting at the embodied user through the interface. The multiplicity of dark affects enunciated by these backend machines and their human administrators is asignified and autopoietically constituted as a zone of control which is perceptually deterritorialised by the user-friendly ethico-aesthetic, reified outside the sensible purview of the user and reterritorialised as part of the scene of empowerment for any actors who have access to software constituting subjective action in the digital and/or the informational capital which they accumulate and circulate in the asignified rhizome of user-friendly design's instrumental technologies.

Not only does this broad cultural shift towards a syntactical, arborescent mode of organisation serve to increasingly striate vital experience like sociality and the expression of identity, it simultaneously reifies social experience in absolute terms of Deleuzian control, subject in Facebook's case to its particular mould of existence, with the profile and other interface elements constantly deforming on a signified level, as the interface changes. Recalling Columbia's point regarding the erasure of the subject/object distinction in user-friendly computers is useful here; Facebook's many ethics scandals and quotidian condition of discursive manipulation serve to remind that this relation exists more as a rhizomatic double bind wherein the use of the user-friendly computer object convokes the sense of an empowered cyborg subjectivity while asignifying a schizoid discursive condition which relates itself automatically to the computer in the multivalent instances of capture and structuration of subjective data, a situation wherein the user is the exploited object of knowledge in untold and multiple contexts operating upon the subject with variable intensity in the creation and maintenance of various data doubles. This destabilises the boundaries of subject/object by actualising both positions concurrently, turning the user into the subject-object of a rhizomatic discourse about themselves, one whose unity is formed through the endless and unpredictable litany of surveillant desires acting upon their data doubles in a manner unified most clearly by the condition of constant biopolitical violence inflicted upon the informational body of the posthuman. A user action may generate many of these relations as information about every kind of user activity is routinely captured and shared between networked computers. These events all exist in an area of imperceptible 'greyness and disenchantment' wherein one never knows whether everything is quite going according to plan at any moment due to complete asignification of process (Guattari 2013: 1; Fuller and Goffey 2012: 11). In this condition of greyness, the asignified theft of financial information due to a banal online purchase made through an unsecure website may take weeks to emerge in a call from the bank. More ambiguous events such as the Cambridge Analytica affair might not have even that minimus of closure and awareness. These examples demonstrate the contingency of exploitation and rhizomatic condition of control haunting digital existence in a user-friendly universe, a phenomenon I propose as schizoveillance. The superpanoptic initiates much of this conception of schizoveillance, but schizoveillance aims to extend Poster's discursive condition of databasing to include the micropolitics of desire, a politics which forms an asignified rhizome of political will and action throughout cyberspace, generating its concrete interface assemblages 'ex nihilo' (Baudrillard 2016) as computer-generated imagery, emerging from publicly unaccountable domains of code and hardware and deterritorialising input back into its unaccountable instrumental plane of asignified control.

IV. Violence and Structure in Cyberspace

While the asignification of instrumentality corresponds to the condition of contingent possibility for much of this cyberspace violence, the signifying grammars of user-friendly design also effect a distinct form of control. To continue with Facebook, we can think of its encoding and representation of content as organised according to a syntax of visual grammar, organising and affecting all social interaction and expression occurring through its interface while utilising all shared content as a means of immaterial labour (Coté and Pybus 2011; Coté 2014) as well as an instrumental component in its asignified political stratum. In this model, to live and use Facebook is to subject oneself to the probing visual grammars of Facebook and tacitly allow for the deterritorialisation of vitalistic experience as proprietary informational capital, much of which is rendered in asignified terms of control.

The representation of content on Facebook initiates a process of algorithmic sortation and a series of constant micropolitical shifts in the control exercised over a subject through observing and selectively reproducing its activity as spectacle for other users, and vice versa; indeed, it is this constant observation which simultaneously provides further grist for the synoptic structure of Facebook, as its representation and dispersion of content is essential to encourage and perpetuate a state of constant and intensive surveillance (Cohen 2008). The convenience offered by Facebook as a tool for social interaction and the signification of identity is contingent upon the concurrent signification of their particular, highly successful, micropolitics of control involving the use of digital interfaces, which Philip Agre (2003) refers to as an ideal medium to implement 'grammars of action', reterritorialising organic and stochastic action into ideally useful forms such as the profile and its selective deterritorialisation of useful informational capital, thereby also maintaining the metastability of Facebook's engine of arbormosis through the unwavering imposition of rigid, digital grammars of action. This imposition conjugates the experience of cyberspace within the signified arborescence of the platform and represents the condition of data doubling as an intrinsic component of the subjectivation of the informational body, and thus the cyborg, entirely within the purview of the rhizomatic and asignified register of algorithms, databases, wholesaling, administration, or even the possible actions of other users, who of course exist on Facebook in ways far beyond their striated representations on the network, as a profile and stream of content. Indeed, the galaxy of asignified actors of variably machinic and human arrangement found throughout the contemporary topology of user-friendly software range, in the case of Facebook, from the innumerable and competing possible actualisations of the interface within the Facebook network as it algorithmically arranges itself for each user, to the manifold uses of the technologically bound posthuman bodies captured by software by Facebook and its corporate partners, ethically wayward administrators, data scientists, unknown third-party hackers, advertisers, and so on; in other words: anyone who may access the asignified rhizome of user-friendly instrumentality by legitimately or illegitimately bypassing the grammatical parameters of its design in order to exercise control over the instrumental infrastructure and/or data of software.

The signification of Facebook's interface design is therefore equally as important for understanding its politics as its asignification, for it represents the imposition of a grammatically defined molar subjectivity which is aligned with Facebook's capitalistic desire to extract subjective information from its users, all of which accords with and entrenches the precepts of user-friendliness. Eli Pariser (2012) has conceptualised the 'filter bubble' as a functional outcome of the arborescent logic of algorithms such as those that allow for Facebook's seductively convenient content sortation, invested primarily in keeping users engaged, using the network, and deterritorialising unto it. Thus, these bubbles operate by reinforcing pre-existing trends regarding user patterns of interaction with different sorts of media, effectively creating a personalised media ecology of self-reinforcing affective content, a personalised regime of signs based entirely upon Facebook's conception of the user's 'self' as a producer-audience object to be controlled and maintained for explicitly capitalistic ends. There have been increasing questions regarding the influence of such filter bubbles on the political polarisation of opposing groups in places where consumption of news media is increasingly through platforms such as Facebook, making their adjudications as to which content they believe a user will like incredibly influential. The vitalistic scope of Facebook, and its commensurately dangerous capacity for the exercise of biopower, has been perhaps laid most bare in the company's 'emotional contagion' scandal, wherein it used its algorithmic sortation to create a more perceptibly negative experience of Facebook's content for a subset of users in order to measure the affect of such a perceptive realignment; unsurprisingly, users who were submerged in this depressing media ecology became more depressed themselves, as measured by the amount and tone of their engagement with the site (Kramer et al. 2014). This naked display of biopower clearly demonstrates the asymmetrical bind of users existing within the user-friendly topology, one which not only exposes users to the asignified rhizome of software politics but imposes its own signifying affect upon users whose experience of becoming-cyborg is increasingly mediated.

Many user-friendly social media networks and other websites have been rightly criticised for a lack of protection within the very design of the networks against subjective manipulation, the exploitation of personal privacy, or other perceptible forms of harassment, abuse and other forms of violence which freely percolate and actualise in a signified, often viscerally abusive, manner. It is allowable content because it clearly serves a capitalistic function of promoting further (violent) discourse, legitimating it as part of the network in a way which apparently supersedes ethical consideration of its subjective impact on others. This recalls Derrida's remarks on the violence of structuralist signification as the enunciation of a fallaciously singular pseudomultiplicity which crushes difference in its pursuit of a perfectly realised structural unity (2002: 2–4), or Butler's conception of the sovereign performative as a category of speech enunciated by the central group subject of a political system which ensures its own survival (1997: 74). In this sense, social networks such as Facebook clearly give away an unfortunate truth of the ethico-aesthetic of cyberspace in their interface design: user-friendly subjectivity follows a molar, majoritarian identity presuming a privilege which is immune to the sorts of abuses typifying the most common negative experiences of social media, such as violently sexist and racist harassment. The continued reification of user-friendly design imposes subjective coordinates which leave its users in a state of becoming-cyborg within a milieu of standardised design that, famously in the case of Twitter's endemic harassment issues, places them in an ideal object position to be the subject of traditional violence by other users. This leaves aside the myriad other ways in which machinic control is more covertly inflected with similar biases as an ontological predicate of their purely coded design, as in the Cambridge Analytica scandal. Small changes to the interface of such networks allowing users to filter their interactions are typically belated and insufficient, while the corporate organisations governing these social media networks, as seen in such areas as their content moderation by humans and algorithms, for example, often reveals forms of exploitation and discriminatory bias as well which operate within the asignified rhizome of the instrumental. In a user-friendly world only the effect is seen, such as being notified that your harassment claim has been rejected by Twitter content moderation, but the process leading to this and possible biases affecting it remain entirely asignified.

We can see then that Facebook provides a clear example of the idiosyncratic style of bureaucratic control allowed by user-friendly design, applied in a brilliant and indisputably successful (albeit socio-politically calamitous) way to social interaction and the representation of identity, emerging in lockstep as part of the continuing march of the capitalist axiomatic to remediate life itself in the efficiently syntactical imagery of software. The convenient and seductively surveillant design of Facebook's software (Cohen 2008), as well as its remediation of an essential element of most human life, provides a means to decode the flows of identity and sociality as data capital. This vector for the data capitalisation of life itself is the dark ethico-aesthetic trajectory which user-friendly software evinces. It is borne out first in the initial theorisations of the world as analogous to unperfected informational signals and redundant noise (Hayles 1999), gradually altered to be redefined as a centralising means of bureaucratic control through information management, and later as a means for the capitalistic remediation of control as part of the stratum of life itself. In this capacity it is put productively to work as an isomorphic reification, or material analogue, to the capitalist axiomatic, with digital information and data as a new quantum flow of decoded, capitalised matter. In the user-friendly topology which characterises the experience of ubiquitously networked software technologies today, the digital codification of experience reterritorialises life as data while simultaneously deterritorialising it into this quantum flow of capital by placing it within an informational 'space of comparison and ... mobile centre of appropriation' (Deleuze and Guattari 1987: 444) in a manner analogous to Deleuze and Guattari's description of the axiomatic system of contemporary capitalism (452–8). This extends and further validates Wendy Chun's astute point that the interface seems to reify ideology (Chun 2011: 59) by suggesting that, if this is true, it has tended to reify the predominant global ideology of capitalism and its collective desire to achieve increasingly immanent deterritorialisations of the planet's resources as a basic condition of cyborg subjectivity. When considering this process in terms of subjectivity and its machinic production, it is useful to consider it as an arbormosis, a remediatory process founded upon principles of arborescence which operate in opposition to the liberatory, experimental subjectivity proposed as chaosmosis by Guattari. Arbormosis constitutes the overcoding process of integrated world capitalism as it traverses the subjective trajectory of becoming-cyborg today, and we are just beginning to see its effects as it warps available subject positions for individuals and groups and infiltrates every ecological register of organisation.

Notes

1. Bifo Berardi defines semiocapitalism as 'the new regime characterized by the fusion of media and capital' and 'a capitalism founded on immaterial labour and the explosion of the infosphere' (2009: 18, 108).
2. For an explanation of the vitalistic turn of mediation, see Kember and Zylinska 2012.
3. Cybernetics represents a particular ethico-aesthetic *aporia* because it captures chaosmosis, the pure state of flux in which any attempt at a singular model inevitably collapses and attempts to arborify the very state of flux itself. Cybernetics thus takes on a certain rhizomatic malleability as it anoints itself a general science for modelling control on a cosmological scale. Its technological realisation has thus introduced an arborescent ethico-aesthetic into the production of subjectivity, the social field, and the libidinal economy writ large.
4. Guattari discusses the importance of bearing the desire for fascism in mind when considering issues throughout any register of organisation: 'The despotism which exists in conjugal or family relationships arises from the same kind of libidinal disposition that exists in the broadest social field. Inversely, it is by no means absurd to approach a number of large scale social problems ... in the light of a micropolitics of desire' (2009b: 156).

5. It is not possible to explore the entire genealogy of user-friendly design in this paper. I have opted to focus upon the less remarked components of user-friendly discourse which pre-date its emergence as a formal ethico-aesthetic in the era of Laurel and Norman, while using Facebook to provide an overview of the composite of rationalisms informing user-friendly design. For an exemplary discussion of their impact and the formalisation of user-friendly design as a cohesive aesthetic movement, see Munster 2006: 117–50. For a broad discussion of bureaucracy as an overcoding force of cybernetics, see Ensmenger 2010. For exemplary accounts of Norman and Laurel's contributions to the user-friendly aesthetic, see Norman 1990 and Laurel 1991.

6. Vis-à-vis user-friendliness, it is useful to consider that Guattari describes the existential territory as an asignified, 'ambiguous' conceptual milieu which foregrounds diverse acts and practices *which can only ever be realised through enactment*: 'These logics, which I call logics of bodies without organs, or logics of existential Territories, have this particularity: that their objects are ontologically ambiguous, they are bifaced object-subjects that can neither be discernibilized nor discursivized as figures represented on a background of coordinates of representation. Thus, they cannot be apprehended from the outside; one can only accept them, take them upon oneself, through an existential transfer' (2013: 40).

7. For accounts of the conscious asignification of elements of the universe which trouble the foundational binary distinctions of cybernetics, see Wiener 2003; Pias 2005; Shannon 2016.

8. Graeber characterises the emergence of the bureaucratic organisation of capitalism as 'the gradual fusion of public and private power into a single entity, rife with rules and regulations whose ultimate purpose is to extract wealth in the form of profits' (2015: 17).

9. For an excellent summation of reporting on the effects of Cambridge Analytica on the 2016 US election, see Grasseger and Krogerus 2016; Hod 2016.

References

Agre, Philip E. (2003) 'Surveillance and Capture: Two Models of Privacy', in Noah Wardrip-Fruin and Nick Montfort (eds), *The New Media Reader*, Cambridge, MA: MIT Press, pp. 737–60.

Baudrillard, Jean (2016) *Why Hasn't Everything Already Disappeared?*, trans. Chris Turner, Calcutta: Seagull Books.

Berardi, Franco 'Bifo' (2009) *Precarious Rhapsody: Semiocapitalism and the Pathologies of the Post-Alpha Generation*, ed. Erik Empson and Stevphen Shukaitis, trans. Arianna Bove, Erik Empson, Michael Goddard, Giuseppina Mecchia, Antonella and Steve Wright, New York: Autonomedia.

Bordo, Susan (1993) *Unbearable Weight: Feminism, Western Culture, and the Body*, Berkeley, CA: University of California Press.

Braidotti, Rosi (2006) *Transpositions: On Nomadic Ethics*, Cambridge: Polity Press.

Butler, Judith (1997) *Excitable Speech: A Politics of the Performative*, London: Routledge.

Butler, Judith (2005) *Giving an Account of Oneself*, New York: Fordham University Press.

Chun, Wendy Hui Kyong (2011) *Programmed Visions: Software and Memory*, Cambridge, MA: MIT Press.

Cohen, Nicole (2008) 'The Valorization of Surveillance: Towards a Political Economy of Facebook', *Democratic Communiqué*, 22:1, pp. 5–22.

Coté, Mark (2014) 'Data Motility: The Materiality of Big Social Data', *Cultural Studies Review*, 20:1, pp. 121–44.

Coté, Mark and Jennifer Pybus (2011) 'Learning to Immaterial Labour 2.0: Facebook and Social Networks', in Michael A. Peters and Ergin Bulut (EDS), *Cognitive Capitalism, Education, and Digital Labour*, New York: Peter Lang.

Deleuze, Gilles and Félix Guattari (1987) *A Thousand Plateaus: Capitalism and Schizophrenia*, trans. Brian Massumi, Minneapolis: University of Minnesota Press.

Deleuze, Gilles and Félix Guattari (1994) *What Is Philosophy?*, trans. Hugh Tomlinson and Graham Burchell, New York: Columbia University Press.

Derrida, Jacques (2002) *Writing and Difference*, trans. Alan Bass, London: Routledge.

Ensmenger, Nathan (2010) *The Computer Boys Take Over: Computers, Programmers, and the Politics of Technical Expertise*, Cambridge, MA: MIT Press.

Fuller, Matthew and Andrew Goffey (2012) *Evil Media*, Cambridge, MA: MIT Press.

Golumbia, David (2009) *The Cultural Logic of Computation*, Cambridge, MA: Harvard University Press.

Graeber, David (2015) *The Utopia of Rules: On Technology, Stupidity, and the Secret Joys of Bureaucracy*, New York: Melville House.

Grasseger, Hannes and Mikael Krogerus (2016) 'The Data that Turned the World Upside Down', *Motherboard*, available at < https://motherboard.vice.com/en_us/article/mg9vvn/how-our-likes-helped-trump-win > (accessed 10 July 2018).

Guattari, Félix (1995) *Chaosmosis: An Ethico-Aesthetic Paradigm*, trans. Paul Bains and Julian Pefanis, Bloomington: Indiana University Press.

Guattari, Félix (2009a) 'The Schizoanalyses', in *Soft Subversions: Texts and Interviews 1977–1985*, ed. Sylvère Lotringer, trans. Chet Wiener and Emily Wittman, Los Angeles: Semiotext(e), pp. 204–25.

Guattari, Félix (2009b) 'Everybody Wants to Be a Fascist', in *Chaosophy: Texts and Interviews 1972–1977*, ed. Sylvère Lotringer, trans. David L. Sweet, Jarred Becker and Taylor Adkins, Los Angeles: Semiotext(e), pp. 154–75.

Guattari, Félix (2009c) 'Capital as the Integral of Power Formations', in *Soft Subversions: Texts and Interviews 1977–1985*, ed. Sylvère Lotringer, trans. Chet Wiener and Emily Wittman, Los Angeles: Semiotext(e), pp. 244–64.

Guattari, Félix (2011) *The Machinic Unconscious*, trans. Taylor Adkins, Los Angeles: Semiotext(e).

Guattari, Félix (2013) *Schizoanalytic Cartographies*, trans. Andrew Goffey, London: Bloomsbury.

Hayles, N. Katherine (1999) *How We Became Posthuman: Virtual Bodies in Cybernetics, Literature, and Informatics*, Chicago: University of Chicago Press.

Hod, Itay (2016) 'How Donald Trump Used Facebook Quizzes to Suppress Hillary Clinton's Vote', *The Wrap*, 30 November, available at < https://www.thewrap.com/ donald-trump-used-facebook-quizzes-suppress-hillary-clintons-vote/ > (accessed 10 July 2018).

Kember, Sarah and Joanna Zylinska (2012) *Life after New Media: Mediation as a Vital Process*, Cambridge, MA: MIT Press.

Kramer, Adam, Jamie Guillory and Jeffrey Hancock (2014) 'Experimental Evidence of Massive-Scale Emotional Contagion through Social Networks', *PNAS*, 111:24, pp. 8788–90.

Laurel, Brenda (1991) *Computers as Theatre*, Reading: Addison-Wesley.

Massumi, Brian (1992) *A User's Guide to Capitalism and Schizophrenia: Deviations from Deleuze and Guattari*, Cambridge, MA: MIT Press.

Munster, Anna (2006) *Materializing New Media: Embodiment in Information Aesthetics*, Hanover, NH: University Press of New England.

Norman, Donald (1990) 'Why Interfaces Don't Work', in Brenda Laurel (ed.), *The Art of Human–Computer Interface Design*, Reading: Addison-Wesley, pp. 209–20.

Pariser, Eli (2012) *The Filter Bubble: How the New Personalized Web Is Changing What We Read and How We Think*, New York: Penguin.

Pias, Claus (2005) 'Analog, Digital, and the Cybernetic Illusion', *Kybernetes*, 34:3/4, pp. 543–50.

Pias, Claus (2016) 'The Age of Cybernetics', in Cybernetics: *The Macy Conferences, 1946–1963 – The Complete Transactions*, Chicago: University of Chicago Press, pp. 1–23.

Pickering, Andy (1995) 'Cyborg History and the World War II Regime', *Perspectives on Science*, 3:1, pp. 1–48.

Poster, Mark (1990), *The Mode of Information: Poststructuralism and Social Contexts*, Chicago: University of Chicago Press.

Shannon, Claude (2016), 'The Redundancy of English', in Claus Pias (ed.), *The Macy Conferences, 1946–1953: The Complete Transactions*, Chicago: University of Chicago Press.

van der Ploeg, Irma (2012) 'The Body as Data in the Age of Information', in Kirstie Ball, Kevin D. Haggerty and David Lyon (eds), *The Routledge Handbook of Surveillance Studies*, New York: Routledge, pp. 176–85.

Wiener, Norbert (1948) *Cybernetics, or the Control and Communication in the Animal and the Machine*, Cambridge, MA: MIT Press.

Wiener, Norbert (1950) *The Human Use of Human Beings: Cybernetics and Society*, Boston: Houghton-Mifflin.

Wiener, Norbert (2003) 'Men, Machines, and the World About', in Noah Wardrip-Fruin and Nick Montfort (eds), *The New Media Reader*, Cambridge, MA: MIT Press, pp. 65–72.

To Fuck with Love Phase II

to fuck with love—
to know the tremor of your flesh within my own—
        feeling of thick sweet juices running wild
        sweat bodies tight and tongue to tongue

I am all those ladies of antiquity enamored of the sun
my cunt is honeycomb we are covered with come and honey
we are covered with each other my skin is the taste of you

    fuck—the fuck of love-fuck—the yes entire—
    love out of ours—the cock in the cunt fuck—
    the fuck of pore into pore—the smell of fuck
    taste it—love dripping from skin to skin—
    tongue at the doorways—cock god in heaven—
    love blooms entire universe—I/you
reflected in the golden mirror we are avatars of
                         Krishna and Radha
      pure love-lust of godhead   beauty unbearable
        carnal incarnate

I am the god-animal, the mindless cuntdeity the hegod-animal
is over me, through me   we are become one total angel
united in fire   united in semen and sweat   united in lovescream

        sacred our acts and our actions
        sacred our parts and our persons

     sacred the sacred cunt!
     sacred the sacred cock!
     miracle!   miracle!   sacred the primal miracle!

      sacred the god-animal, twisting and wailing

          sacred the beautiful fuck

        Lenore Kandel, Feminist Beat Poet

Deleuze and Guattari Studies 12.4 (2018): 595
DOI: 10.3366/dlgs.2018.0334
© The Estate of Lenore Kandel
www.euppublishing.com/dlgs

Love, Consent, and Arousal: Deterritorialising Virtual Sex

Cheri Lynne Carr   LaGuardia Community College, CUNY

Abstract

A feminist-inspired, Deleuzo-Guattarian conception of love can be a model of designing virtual reality experiences that pursue their liberating rather than enslaving trajectories.

Keywords: virtual, feminism, love, sex, pornography

> Erotic content should have the complete opposite effect to creating a zombie nation of VR porn slaves. The best pornography has the ability to teach, to inspire us to reach out to another human being and explore their body, desires and pleasures.

> (Erika Lust 2015)

I. Fascism of the (Virtual) Self

In his short 1990 essay 'Postscript on the Societies of Control', Deleuze outlines the contours of what he saw as the new forms of control rapidly replacing what Foucault had identified as forms of subjectivation based on discipline. While disciplinary societies were predicated on enclosure (the school, the factory, the hospital, the prison) – and so operated according to clear practices of limitation of freedom, the societies of control operate through 'free-floating' control that offers an appearance of freedom but in actuality repeats in a more refined, subterranean form mechanisms of control 'equal to the harshest of confinements' (Deleuze 1992: 4). What Deleuze was anticipating were pervasive, technological networks of control such as can be seen

Deleuze and Guattari Studies 12.4 (2018): 597–611
DOI: 10.3366/dlgs.2018.0335
© Edinburgh University Press
www.euppublishing.com/dlgs

today in phenomena like widespread reliance on smart phone access to the Internet 'information superhighway'.[1] Though this technology seems to offer unlimited freedom and access to knowledge, it comes with increased surveillance, logarithmic regulation, pervasive marketing, and a creeping sense of its social and professional indispensability. Virtual reality (VR) technologies are the most recent unfolding of this type of power: they are a burgeoning regime within the societies of control, appropriating and reterritorialising desire in ways that serve to fortify the dominant capitalist agenda by habituating the ego to an internalisation of its neoliberal value system, creating an assemblage that reproduces and intensifies fascism within the self (Conley 2009: 36, 30–1; Evans and Reid 2013: 2). Mainstream VR pornography, for instance, channels desire through identification with repressive, molar forms of sexuality that ultimately reproduce sexual objectification and consumerism while limiting the pleasures of sexual and social becomings that bodies are capable of exploring (Fox and Bale 2018: 405). Yet, despite the emphasis on the dystopian possibilities attendant on the rise of the VR 'metaverse' in fictional depictions of the near-future – from *Neuromancer* and *Snow Crash* in the 1990s to *Black Mirror* and *Ready Player One* in the late 2010s – Deleuze argues in the 'Postscript' that regimes within the societies of control are neither good nor bad. Rather, they have within them a confrontation between 'liberating and enslaving forces' (Deleuze 1992: 4). Identifying and distinguishing the liberating forces operating within VR from the enslaving ones is crucial for refining a set of analytical tools and design practices that uses the uniquely promising features of VR for supporting deterritorialisations of the self and opens explorations of new terrains of pleasure, for increasing our capacity for affection, and for setting the stage for a freer world.

II. What Can Virtual Reality Do?

Ken Hillis, writing back in 1996, defined virtual reality as 'the technical means for access to the "parallel" disembodied and increasingly networked visual "world" named cyberspace' (1996: 70).[2] This apt but bloodless description belies the raw intensity of VR experiences. While VR is typically described as not 'real' in the way we normally mean that term – that it is an artificial construct, 'bits cobbled together to produce sounds and images that we observe' – it *feels* real in a way that is hard to understand until it has been experienced (Lemley and Volokh fothcoming 2018: 3). People in VR environments physiologically respond to actions done to them in VR. People who experience their

VR body being harmed respond with skin conductance and heart rate levels as if their physical body were actually being harmed (Hägni et al. 2008). The results are replicable even when the person is male and their VR body is female (Slater et al. 2010). Indeed, Brian Massumi has argued that the problem with the term 'virtual reality' is that it tends 'rapidly to degrade into a synonym for "artificial" or "simulation", used with tiresome predictability as antonyms for "reality"' (1998: 16). In response, Massumi suggests using the Deleuzo-Guattarian term 'virtual' without the 'reality' tag – not because the virtual is thought to have no reality but because its reality is assumed, the only question being what mode it takes. For Deleuze and Guattari, the virtual is 'the mode of reality implicated in the emergence of new potentials' (Massumi 1998: 16). It resides within the actual, on the surface of material relationships, as a residue or excess of freedom that, when accessed, can foment actual change and transformation. VR's power to produce transformations is likewise due to its ability to unlink and shift perception from the perceiving body – allowing consciousness to dissolve the experience of static identity and essentiality that serve to bias and limit it. It is because of VR's unique ability to dissolve and reroute habitual modes of relation between the body and the mind that VR technologies have shown promise in easing chronic pain and in diminishing the symptoms of post-traumatic stress disorder (Shahrbanian et al. 2009; Oneal et al. 2008; Hoffman et al. 2001; Rothbaum et al. 2001). This capability is also why VR technologies might be seen as a potential ally to the work of Deleuze and Guattari's schizoanalysis: the realness of VR experiences allows us to viscerally encounter the arbitrariness of some of our and our culture's most cherished distinctions. The distinction between the mind and the body is one example. The fixity of gendered experiences is another.

Yet, as a result of this same capacity, VR technologies – more so than other forms of technology – offer engineers, marketers, and designers dramatically increased power to manipulate emotions, to uncritically reinscript oppressive norms, and to increase capitalist and hegemonic control over the body. This is particularly visible in the more lucrative side of VR technology – gaming and pornography – where deployments of VR have tended to amplify long-established misogynistic cultural ideals, creating a potentially (and often actually) traumatising experience for women.[3] VR can amplify these widespread, destructive practices and biases because it removes the need to bridge the gap between expression and perception, resulting in the erosion of the critical apparatus people have the capacity to bring to their engagements with others and the world. As VR entrepreneur Chris Milk, in a now-infamous 2016 TED Talk argues, VR will be the last medium because 'your consciousness is the medium' – VR gives the artist 'a unique, direct path into your senses, your emotions, even your body'.[4] While Milk tries to emphasise the potential of VR experiences to inspire awe and forge unmediated connections between artists and viewers, this 'unique, direct path' into your body is fraught with danger. Not only can it cause vertigo (or cybersickness) if the experience is not carefully orchestrated with regard to how it is moving the viewer through space, which Milk acknowledges, it also requires a willingness to put one's body into the hands of another, which Milk does not seem to consider as an inherent problem of access. But this requirement is considerable, particularly for many women, LGBTQ+ people, and people of colour, whose historical oppression and abuse at the hands of others makes trust in even the good intentions of those in positions of power troubled. And while it would be hyperbolic to suggest that Milk's failure to sense this danger is an instance of rape culture in new technology, it nevertheless seems fair to say that his and other VR designers' priorities have not been in actively resisting this culture and may in some instances be complicit with it.

Awareness of the problem of rape culture in new technology has become more pronounced in the wake of both the 2014 #Gamergate harassment controversy and the first allegations of sexual assault in a VR multi-player gaming platform made in October 2016.[5] Assault in VR halts the movement of deterritorialisation returning consciousness to the body by creating the object of its assault even if no object is there. A similar phenomenon accompanies harassment, discrimination, and exclusionary design – the deterritorialising effects of VR are nullified by trapping the viewer in their (recreated) individualised body. So, while the VR viewer may have a range of actions available to try, such as looking around Paris in 360 degrees from the comfort of their own living room, experiencing everyday life through the eyes of a refugee child or a woolly mammoth, and walking about or teleporting within the virtual environment of There or *InWorldz*, it is important to remember that the VR experience is meticulously designed, engineered, and constructed to control and profit from the viewer's experience. The widespread, background normalisation of sexual objectification and violence in the larger entertainment culture that is being translated into VR operates to intensify these control mechanisms – and it is these that a Deleuzo-Guattarian analysis could be deployed to undo. The Oedipal illusion that the drive to sexual assault belongs to represents a repressive, fascistic investment of desire that is bound up with the economic prerogatives of capitalism. But if desire is to be liberated in the future, where virtual worlds can be commodified and subjected to the same molar categories of sexuality limiting our reality today, analysing the Oedipal and capitalist investments inherent not just in the content but also in the design of VR technologies becomes imperative as they function as the condition of the possibility of experiencing the vertiginous deterritorialisation VR offers.[6]

Currently, the design choices made within mainstream VR production have emphasised immersiveness over interactivity and emotional manipulation over the creation of spaces of open play.[7] Within VR pornography, the majority of available experiences are simple, mechanical, male point of view-style in which the viewer is unable to touch, feel, or interact with others or even the virtual images. This creates an entirely voyeuristic – though impressively immersive – experience defined by the narrowest of male, heterosexual gazes. Erotic filmmaker Erika Lust, remarking on this phenomenon, worries that it will produce 'porn-consuming zombie junkies, sitting next to our lovers in the same bed, but not ever speaking to or touching one another' (2015). Lust's worry thus echoes Deleuze's worry about the societies of control: that VR provides the illusion of freedom and connection while not providing any of the material conditions for real freedom or connection – perhaps even undermining the few avenues for freedom and connection that people have.

Despite these worries, Lust sees herself and other female, queer directors as leading a charge to change the way the porn industry orients itself towards VR. Lust and others seek to imbue greater creativity, interactivity, and more inclusive, less narrow narratives of arousal into virtual sex. Her work and attention to the issues of diversity, access, and consent are timely, thoughtful, and laudable, yet Lust's project and those like it that – in the vein of Wilhelm Reich's work – see freedom from sexual repression as the key to the development of a healthy ego and relationships, will only be able to deploy piecemeal and superficial 'fixes' to VR design if they do not also address the confinement of the body within the ideal of the individual subject itself. For Deleuze's project in the 'Postscript' as well as in his work with Guattari in *Capitalism and Schizophrenia*, the truth of fascism is that it is an expression of the desire for repression of one's own multiple, imbricated, and fluid selves. In order for Lust's project to succeed as radically as she would like, a Deleuzo-Guattarian analysis of capitalist investment in individual identity that seeks to discover how desire is constructed through the design of VR interfaces is necessary.

In the 'Postscript', Deleuze leaves to the younger generation of thinkers, those who will be operating within the societies of control, to discover 'what they're being made to serve' and the 'new weapons' that must be forged in resistance (1992: 7). Mainstream VR today operates to further the movement towards individualisation embedded in capitalist requirements of breaking apart groups for the purpose of creating a larger market and making users willingly feed more money to those who control access. While corporations seek to control by diverting the affects through the production of 'brand loyalty', to arouse consumer need by manufacturing desire through the manipulation of fantasy into a pre-made phallic economy, the 'joys of marketing' Deleuze found so worrying in the 'Postscript' seek to co-opt or appropriate love – to incorporate our desires and affects into the corporate agenda, to manufacture gratefulness for our debt. The result is the detachment of desire from its unanticipatable project of deterritorialisation by reterritorialising desire onto the brand. But perhaps today the weapon we might forge to resist the 'joys of marketing' is just that: love.

III. The Art of Loving Counter to All Forms of Fascism

Christian Kerslake argues that love is the privileged form of desire in Deleuze's work because desire is not desire for a particular object, it is the desire to be 'drawn into' another world expressed by that object (2010: 79, 51). John Protevi goes as far as to suggest that Deleuze is only ever thinking about love – insofar as his thinking is always 'linked rather directly to desire, to alterity, to getting outside oneself', even if 'love' is not his most widely recognised concept (2003: 183). For Protevi, love is an experiment engaged in to provoke a novel occurrence, to enter the virtual, and thereby open the actual to the creation of 'new bodies, new flows, new affects' (2003: 184, 193). For Hannah Stark and Timothy Laurie, love is clearly part of the Deleuzo-Guattarian project of critiquing identity. In a discussion drawing on connections between Deleuze and Negri's work, they write, 'love composes singular persons into joyful collective unities' (2017: 71), resisting the popular sense of love as private and singular that is visible in what bell hooks, following M. Scott Peck, calls 'cathexis' ([2001] 2018: 3–4). Love as cathexis is the feeling of profound connection with another person that is achieved through concentrating mental and emotional energy into that person as an individual, which hooks finds deeply problematic for the actuality of loving (hooks [2001] 2018: 3). It coincides with what John Protevi calls 'Oedipalized love' and contrasts with 'schizo' or revolutionary love (2003: 188). While Oedipal love is 'personal, exclusively differentiated, fixed in meaning, guilty, and familial', schizo love is 'material (not representational), social (not familial), and multiple (not personal)' (Protevi 2003: 188–9). Unlike Oedipal love or cathexis, schizo love is not fascistic, not a form of mastery over the lover or over chance. Rather than think of love in terms of feeling, of merging, or of recognition, for Deleuze and Guattari the love encounter 'is a process by which the self is undone' (Stark 2012: 108). However, for Stark 'the depersonalisation which love entails eradicates the subject while retaining both subjectivity and subjective experience' (2012: 108). This point that subjectivity and experience are retained in the dissolution of the rigid notion of the individualised subject is crucial not only for realising the socially and politically transformative power of love, but also for supporting the special relevance of VR experiences for experimenting with schizo love. Love for Stark maintains consistency while simultaneously supporting the experience of pursuing lines of flight. In *A Thousand Plateaus* the ideas of becoming imperceptible and making oneself a body without organs vis-à-vis experimentation are mediated through the encounter with virtuality – but Deleuze and Guattari's insight is that there are pitfalls to avoid in such experimentation, such as whether the experimentation need fully 'engage' and put the body in danger or if it can operate like a thought experiment – safer and more abstract. VR seems to offer an interesting third way – a way to fully engage the experiment with lines of flight that (at least if designed well) maintains consistency for subjective experience rather than threatening full schizophrenia.

VR, it seems, holds out the potential to become a privileged space in which to experiment with schizo love, with getting outside oneself, and to reclaim desire's deterritorialising, depersonalising project while resisting the Oedipalised, familial love limiting our capacity for pleasure. For Deleuze and Guattari, accessing the transformational power of the virtual to catalyse moving beyond the actual – that is, resisting the present – goes hand in hand with the dissolution or deterritorialisation of the individualised self (though not subjective experience, as Stark points out). Since VR has the capacity to deterritorialise habitual assemblages and deindividuate the self, it can thereby be a force for the proliferation of pleasure and the increase of material, bodily flows, increasing our capacity for affection. This helps to justify the emphasis on pornography in VR: as Fox and Bale put it, 'the sexuality of the contemporary West is an impoverished and constrained refraction of a body's potential for physical, emotional and/or cognitive intensifications' (2018: 394).

Sexuality is linked to the Virtual. We should shift 'to a radical approach to sex and sexualities education for children and adults that aims for the "re-sexualisation of everyone"' (Fox and Bale 2018: 406). But it is not as simple as a sex-positive story might propose. As Jessica Ringrose, Marnina Gonick, Emma Renold, and Lisa Weems's work has shown:

> for young women today in post-feminist cultures the display of a certain kind of sexual knowledge, sexual practice and sexual agency has become normative – indeed, a 'technology of sexiness' has replaced 'innocence' and 'virtue' as the commodity that young women are required to offer in the heterosexual marketplace. (Ringrose et al. 2009: 2–3)

The challenge of designing for VR in ways that sustain its capability of allying with schizo love is to resist participating in the production of truth about sex, which leads inevitably to the rigidification of identity categories. We can, on the other hand, approach VR as a potential site of deterritorialisation of the subject – of the creation of openness onto new worlds – and work to make VR life-affirming rather than life-negating by asking how we can love virtually, how we can make schizo love in VR. And because of VR's unique qualities, we can approach VR as a site for the creation of and experimentation with schizo love by advocating for and supporting the design of VR in ways that increase our capacity for affection, that increase our capacity for activity, freedom, and connection rather than decrease it, that engineer the VR experience with the model of schizo love as deterritorialisation in mind: 'our love addresses itself to this libidinal property of our lover, to either close himself off or open up to more spacious worlds, to masses and large aggregates' (Deleuze and Guattari 2004: 294). To do this, the proposal here is to use the Deleuzo-Guattarian ethical framework of resistance to fascism proposed by Foucault in the Preface to *Anti-Oedipus* as a fruitful way of thinking through liberatory practices of VR pornography as a deployment of viral, virtual love.

IV. To Fuck (Virtually) with Love

In the preface to *Anti-Oedipus*, Foucault (1983) identifies seven principles that guide the art of living counter to all forms of fascism. The following five principles of the art of loving through VR pornography are derived from Foucault's. Deterritorialising virtual sex necessitates design that is anti-fascistic, encourages freedom, arouses the player, resists sexual and identitarian categorisations, and increases our capacities for affection. Such practices of schizo love in virtual reality, the hope is, can lay the groundwork for the affective shift needed for revolutionary shifts in actual reality as well.

Schizo love is anti-fascistic and non-controlling. In VR, to love would mean to refuse to use the technology as a platform for capitalist control and profit divorced from social responsibility. This does not imply that VR pornography cannot be a business. One example of a highly successful and influential business model based on a proto form of anti-fascistic love is the movement of feminist sex toy and educational stores begun in the 1970s – in particular Joani Blank's San Francisco-based Good Vibrations. Blank's approach to her store was influenced by the Briarpatch philosophy of business. For 'Briars', as practitioners are known, retail business can and should support socially conscious community engagement. Briars practised open-bookkeeping, actively shared knowledge and marketing strategies, kept prices low, sourced their products locally where possible, and used profits to futher the educational and activist missions of their stores. At Good Vibrations, Blank utilised these strategies to engender 'credibility and respect from customers who felt good about shopping' there, helping to simultaneously spread the message of sex positivity and shape what is now a $15 billion industry.[8]

Schizo love promotes freedom. In VR, to love would mean to avoid censorship. As Katerina Liskova summarises the 'war' between anti-porn and sex-positive feminists, while anti-porn feminists (such as MacKinnon and Dworkin) 'rallied for legal action with the ultimate aim of redefining pornography as the degradation and dehumanisation of women', sex-positive feminists diagnosed this attitude as a form of censorship that hurt women far more than pornography. After a Canadian court decision against pornography, praised by MacKinnon as a victory for women, led to criminal charges being brought against a Toronto-based gay and lesbian bookstore for selling a lesbian erotic magazine, 'the legal restriction of pornography proposed by pro-censorship feminists proved, ironically, to actually silence women, particularly those who challenged the expected sex-gender-desire coherence' (Liskova 2009). Promoting freedom also means that the technology should not be used for advertising, rhetoric, or manipulation. Rather than censorship or advertising to manipulate, VR designers should focus on arousal – on opening new avenues for desire to assemble.

Schizo love arouses. In VR pornography, to love would mean to 'design for eroticism'. VR porn could lead the way offering real action and interaction rather than emphasising immersiveness, systematisation, or pre-programming. A real interaction might be an extension of the teledildonics market to haptic wear, for instance. Where the haptic wear is interfacing with an AI, biofeedback systems could replace pre-programmed ones. Design should allow for multiple possible paths for exploration and emphasise play and foreplay, approach consent as a process, and support mobile, nomadic arrangements rather than limit players to 'logical' ones. The queer VR pornographic filmmakers of MetaverseXXX are an example of a group working to offer an alternative to the often violent, explicit, and degrading imagery in pornography by emphasising real play. Their insight is that acting – when you translate it to the VR experience – is very 'cheesy', so their strategy is to encourage their actors to just engage in play, without narrative; They employ a concept of 'designing for eroticism' that offers multiple paths of arousal as alternatives to narratives tied to a specific image of masculinity that they perceived to be toxic to genuine eroticism. They are thereby avoiding the negative in favour of offering something positive and multiple that encourages difference over uniformity, flows over unities, and mobile arrangements over systems.

Schizo love resists categorising and encourages becoming. In VR, this would mean designing for openness to and encouragement of increasingly diffuse queer/non-binary VR experiences. Designing an open space for the proliferation of sexualities, while also resisting their rigidification and categorisation, would mean encouraging increasingly diffuse queer VR experiences. Rather than categorising these bodies, it would favour designing for the possibility of bodies becoming other in the process. For deterritorialising the self, it would mean designing experiences that confuse the molar categories that have structured our ways of understanding ourselves: gender, for instance (in pornography we might design 'avatars' that express the possibility of a sexual spectrum, so our possibilities of experiencing pleasure are less circumscribed by our bodies and current imaginaries). Indeed, as Deleuze and Guattari write, 'all love then must be a material dismantling of the organism and the subject to reach the body, that is, a reshuffling of the stereotyped patterns and triggers of Oedipal living': 'Make the body without organs of consciousness and love. Use love and consciousness to abolish subjectification' (1987: 134). Identities are, in Deleuze's view, always and necessarily oppressive. Sexuality is a matter of becoming and cannot be fully grasped in terms of the organic structure of human bodies or the psychic positions derived from the Oedipus complex. This is what allows Deleuze to claim that sexuality is badly explained by 'the binary organisation of sexes and no better [explained] by a bi-sexed organisation of each of the two' (1987: 278). Sexuality as becoming cannot be confined to a binary precisely because becoming has the power of connecting terms that are entirely heterogeneous, bringing together humans, animals, molecules, across natural kingdoms. If in sexuality everything is a matter of differences, then differences are exactly what cannot be reduced to the logic of binary oppositions. This is the Deleuzian way of affirming that having a sexual life is not having a sexual identity.[9]

Finally, schizo love should expand our capacity for affection. The design of VR must prioritise developing avenues to augment the capability of acting–offering real action rather than the illusion of action. Instead of focusing on immersiveness, it should focus on expanding activity and interaction–not just how it can affect the individual viewer. Indeed, it should resist the movement to encapsulate the individual that is ubiquitous in the hardware of VR technology and instead seek avenues of interface expansion that support becoming less of an individual. This goal can also be pursued in VR software design. So, we might delve deeper into affective processes involved in forging connection. For this, we could turn to Claire Hemmings's concept of 'affective solidarity' (2012) to explore how digital connections and mediation between girls and women have enabled new forms of solidarity. In VR pornography, this would mean designing for affective contagion that leads to new affective assemblages becoming translated to the actual. As Foucault (1983) writes, it is the connection of desire to reality that possesses revolutionary force. Pleasure in VR triggers a 'group' dynamic–if the players are laughing and clapping, then this triggers in the viewer the desire to laugh and clap–the connection of desire to reality through the infectiousness of joy is the revolutionary force they seek to wield (MetaverseXXX). This would be schizo love in the world:

> But to move from knowing more to valuing that knowledge requires a shift of some kind in this scene, a shift that will invariably call for critique. I suggest that an affective shift must first occur to produce the struggle that is the basis of alternative standpoint knowledge and politics.... . Affect might flood one's being and change not only how the house and its circumstances are experienced and understood, but how everything else is seen and understood too, from this time on. (Hemmings 2012: 157)

V. Game Over? Continue. Yes/No

In conclusion, the technological breakthroughs of VR offer a potential ally to the project of deterritorialisation and deindividuation if designed in conjunction with a robust understanding of a Deleuzo-Guattarian 'schizo' love. By developing a path of resistance to domination in

VR pornography – an industry that has historically exploited women and the vulnerable for material gain – we can also develop a path of resistance through the use of VR as well: one that goes part of the way to addressing concerns in new technology about rape culture, the increased power of new technology to manipulate emotions, the uncritical repetition of oppressive norms, and increased capitalist and hegemonic control over the body, leading to the separation of people from their capacity to act.

Notes

1. The term 'information superhighway' refers to all our interwoven forms of digital communication. It was coined by Tennessee's then-Senator Al Gore, Jr. in a 1978 address to his Senate 'futures group'. See Hale and Scanlon 1999: 100.
2. Use of the term 'cyberspace' to refer to a shared virtual world was coined by William Gibson in a 1982 short story called 'Burning Chrome'. However, since 'cyberspace' has commonly come to be understood as synonymous with the Internet it is no longer the preferred term used to refer specifically to the collective VR shared space. Currently, the term 'metaverse', coined by Neal Stephenson in his 1992 novel *Snow Crash*, is preferred.
3. The game 'Dead or Alive Xtreme 3 [VR]' has received extensive criticism in the world of gaming journalism as a result of its incorporation of active sexual harassment as part of the gameplay. Though 'Dead or Alive' is a particularly egregious example, the (almost exclusively female) journalists and social scientists publishing on it have been careful to emphasise that it is not an isolated example. Much of gaming culture is built on the objectification of women. When those practices and value system are translated into a first-person VR experience, it becomes even more troubling, as is evidenced by Outlaw and Duckles's ongoing research into virtual harassment, in which they claim that almost 50 per cent of women who regularly use VR have encountered virtual sexual harassment or assault (see Outlaw and Duckles 2017, 2018; Buchleitner 2018; Frank 2016; Bort 2016; MacLellan 2016).
4. Milk seems to be referencing Marshall McLuhan's oft-quoted insight that 'the medium is the message', that is, that the predominant 'media defined *the nature of knowledge in any given epoch*' (Taylor and Harris 2008: 88). See also McLuhan and Fiore [1967] 2001. What sort of epochal knowledge VR might define is a question worthy of exploration. On Deleuze and Guattari's account, this knowledge would likely be tightly controlled by capitalist interests.
5. Rape culture can broadly be defined as a socio-cultural context in which an aggressive male sexuality is eroticised and seen as a 'healthy', 'normal', and 'desired' part of sexual relations (Herman 1984). A rape culture is one in which sexual assault is not only seen as *inevitable* in some contexts, but *desirable* and *excusable* as well (Mendes 2015: 5–6). This is because women are constructed as *enjoying* being aggressively pursued, and in some cases, *overpowered* by men. Women are also seen as *deserving* or *provoking* rape by failing to perform a chaste femininity, or for sending out signals to men that they are 'up for it', regardless of how much they protest (see Buchwald et al. 2005; Valenti 2007). These so-called 'signals' include staying out late at night, drinking alcohol, flirting with men, wearing 'provocative' clothing, or being sexually active (see Bonnes 2013; Meyer 2010).

6. The optimism surrounding VR in the tech world mirrors in some ways early cyber-feminist optimism concerning technological innovation towards the more social/culturally critical technofeminist recognition that uncritically embracing or hailing the possibilities that the virtual world would empower women and make them less dependent on biology, more empowered and freer to transcend gender stereotypes and sexism, fails to address that technology does not exist in a vacuum: that VR disembodied subjectivities exist within a set of social relations to which they must return, and that the very virtual worlds themselves are constructed through the prejudices and values of their users – who happen to be predominantly male. For cyber-feminism (a term coined in 1994 by Sadie Plant, director of the Cybernetic Culture Research Unit at the University of Warwick in the UK, to describe the work of feminists interested in theorising, critiquing, and exploiting the Internet, cyberspace, and new media technologies in general), see Plant 1996. For critique of early cyberfeminist optimism, see Wajcman 2004.

7. As a result, in part, of the voices of women in VR design, there has been a small movement to support VR platforms that offer more shared, interactive experiences, though the promise of these has so far exceeded the execution. However, even in the games and platforms that emphasise social interaction and 'sandbox' play, such as with QuiVr, their design has in often subtle ways left open the door to sexual harassment and abuse. It took a high-profile incident of sexual assault on the QuiVr platform for the designers of the game to introduce a 'power move' that makes would-be assailants disappear from the viewing area. It is widespread experiences like these that Outlaw and Duckles's research compiles.

8. The worldwide sex toy industry, once a niche operation, is now worth over US$15 billion annually and is primarily run by and for women. For more data and extensive demographic information, see the Statistic Brain Research Institute's 2017 report on the sex toy industry at < https://www.statisticbrain.com/sex-toy-statistics/ > (accessed 20 July 2018).

9. Sexual difference in Deleuze and Guattari has been discussed at length in Marrati 2006 and Colebrook 2000.

References

Bonnes, Stephanie (2013) 'Gender and Racial Stereotyping in Rape Coverage', *Feminist Media Studies*, 13:2, pp. 208–27.

Bort, Julie (2016) 'A Virtual Reality Game that Allows Characters to Sexually Assault Women is Slated for Release in Japan', *Business Insider Nordic*, 30 August, available at < https://nordic.businessinsider.com/sexual-assault-video-game-japan-2016-8 > (accessed 20 July 2018).

Buchleitner, Jessica (2018) 'When Virtual Reality Feels Real, so Does the Sexual Harassment', *Reveal*, 5 April, available at < https://www.revealnews.org/article/when-virtual-reality-feels-real-so-does-the-sexual-harassment/ > (accessed 20 July 2018).

Buchwald, Emilie, Pamela Fletcher and Martha Roth (eds) (2005) *Transforming a Rape Culture*, Minneapolis: Milkweed Editions.

Colebrook, Claire (2000) 'Is Sexual Difference a Problem?', in Ian Buchanan and Claire Colebrook (eds), *Deleuze and Feminist Theory*, Edinburgh: Edinburgh University Press, pp. 110–27.

Conley, Verena Andermatt (2009) 'Thirty-Six Thousand Forms of Love: The Queering of Deleuze and Guattari', in Chrysanthi Nigianni and Merl Storr (eds), *Deleuze and Queer Theory*, Edinburgh: Edinburgh University Press, pp. 24–36.

Deleuze, Gilles (1992) 'Postscript on the Societies of Control', *October*, 59:Winter, pp. 3–7.

Deleuze, Gilles and Félix Guattari (2004), *Anti-Oedipus: Capitalism and Schizophrenia*, trans. Robert Hurley, Mark Seem and Helen R. Lane, Minneapolis: University of Minnesota Press.

Deleuze, Gilles and Félix Guattari (1987) *A Thousand Plateaus: Capitalism and Schizophrenia*, trans. Brian Massumi, Minneapolis: University of Minnesota Press.

Evans, Brad and Julian Reid (eds) (2013) *Deleuze and Fascism*, Abingdon: Routledge.

Foucault, Michel (1983) 'Preface', in *Anti-Oedipus: Capitalism and Schizophrenia*, trans. Robert Hurley, Mark Seem and Helen R. Lane, Minneapolis: University of Minnesota Press, pp. xi–xiv.

Fox, Nick J. and Clare Bale (2018) 'Bodies, Pornography and the Circumscription of Sexuality: A New Materialist Study of Young People's Sexual Practices', *Sexualities*, 21:3, pp. 393–409.

Frank, Allegra (2016) 'With VR Mode Dead or Alive Goes from creepy to Harassment', *Polygon*, 30 August, available at < https://www.polygon.com/2016/8/30/12710076/dead-or-alive-vr-mode-harassment > (accessed 30 July 2018).

Hägni, Karin, Kynan Eng, Marie-Claude Hepp-Reymond, Lisa Holper, Birgit Keisker, Ewa Siekierka and Daniel C. Kiper (2008) 'Observing Virtual Arms that You Imagine Are Yours Increases the Galvanic Skin Response to an Unexpected Threat', *PLoS ONE*, 3:8, e3082, available at < http://journals.plos.org/plosone/article?id=10.1371/journal.pone.0003082 > (accessed 20 July 2018).

Hale, Constance and Jessie Scanlon (1999) *Wired Style: Principles of English Usage in the Digital Age*, New York: Broadway.

Hemmings, Claire (2012) 'Affective Solidarity: Feminist Reflexivity and Political Transformation', *Feminist Theory*, 13:2, pp. 147–61.

Herman, Dianne (1984) 'The Rape Culture', in Jo Freeman (ed.), *Women: A Feminist Perspective*, Mountain View, CA: Mayfield, pp. 45–53.

Hillis, Ken (1996), 'A Geography of the Eye: The Technologies of Virtual Reality', in Rob Shields (ed.), *Cultures of Internet: Virtual Spaces, Real Histories, Living Bodies*, London: Sage, pp. 70–99.

Hoffman, Hunter G., David R. Patterson, Gretchen Carrougher, Sam R. Sharar (2001), 'The Effectiveness of Virtual Reality Based Pain Control with Multiple Treatments', *The Clinical Journal of Pain*, 17:3, pp. 229–35.

hooks, bell [2001] (2018) *All About Love*, New York: HarperCollins.

Kerslake, Christian (2010) 'Desire and the Dialectics of Love: Deleuze, Canguilhem, and the Philosophy of Desire', in Leen De Bolle (ed.), *Deleuze and Psychoanalysis: Philosophical Essays on Deleuze's Debate with Psychoanalysis*, Leuven: Leuven University Press, pp. 50–81.

Lemley, Mark A. and Eugene Volokh (forthcoming 2018) 'Law, Virtual Reality, and Augmented Reality', *University of Pennsylvania Law Review*, 166:4, available at < https://papers.ssrn.com/sol3/papers.cfm?abstract_id=2933867 > (accessed 20 July 2018).

Liskova, Katerina (2009) 'Feminist Sex Wars', in Jodi O'Brien (ed.), *Encyclopedia of Gender and Society*, Thousand Oaks, CA: Sage, pp. 316–18.

Lust, Erika (2015) 'How Virtual Reality Could Change Porn for the Better', Fortune, 29 July, available at < http://fortune.com/2015/07/29/virtual-reality-porn/ > (accessed 20 July 2018).

MacLellan, Lila (2016) 'Virtual Reality is a Hotbed for Sexual Assault', *Quartz*, 1 November, available at < https://qz.com/823575/virtual-realitys-female-gamers-say-the-gaming-world-is-rife-with-sexual-harassment-and-it-feels-worse-in-3d/ > (accessed 20 July 2018).

McLuhan, Marshall and Quentin Fiore [1967] (2001) *The Medium is the Massage*, Berkeley, CA: Gingko Press.

Marrati, Paola (2006) 'Time and Affects: Deleuze on Gender and Sexual Difference', *Australian Feminist Studies*, 21:51, pp. 313–25.

Massumi, Brian (1998) 'Sensing the Virtual, Building the Insensible', Stephen Perrella (ed.), *Hypersurface Architecture*, 68:5/6, pp. 16–24.

Mendes, Kaitlynn (2015) *SlutWalk: Feminism, Activism, and Media*, Basingstoke: Palgrave Macmillan.

Meyer, Anneke (2010) '"Too Drunk to Say No": Binge Drinking, Rape and the *Daily Mail*', *Feminist Media Studies*, 10:1, pp. 19–34.

Milk, Chris (2016), 'The Birth of Virtual Reality as an Art Form', *TED2016*, February, available at < https://www.ted.com/talks/chris_milk_the_birth_of_virtual_reality_as_an_art_form/transcript?language=en > (accessed 20 July 2018).

Oneal, Brent J., David R. Patterson, Maryam Soltani, Aubriana Teeley and Mark P. Jensen (2008) 'Virtual Reality Hypnosis in the Treatment of Chronic Neuropathic Pain: A Case Report', *International Journal of Clinical and Experimental Hypnosis*, 56:4, pp. 451–62.

Outlaw, Jessica and Beth Duckles (2017) 'Why Women Don't Like Social Virtual Reality: A Study of Safety, Usability, and Self-Expression in Social Virtual Reality', *The Extended Mind*, available at < https://static1.squarespace.com/static/56e315ede321404618e90757/t/5afca0716d2a73e7b3c77f28/1526505624385/The+Extended+Mind_Why+Women+Don%27t+Like > (accessed 20 July 2018).

Outlaw, Jessica and Beth Duckles (2018) 'Virtual Harassment: The Social Experience of 600+ Regular Virtual Reality (VR) Users', *The Extended Mind Blog*, 4 April, available at < https://extendedmind.io/blog/2018/4/4/virtual-harassment-the-social-experience-of-600-regular-virtual-reality-vrusers > (accessed 20 July 2018).

Plant, Sadie (1996) 'On the Matrix: Cyberfeminist Simulations', in Rob Shields (ed.), *Cultures of Internet: Virtual Spaces, Real Histories, Living Bodies*, London: Sage, pp. 170–83.

Protevi, John (2003) 'Love', in Paul Patton and John Protevi (eds), *Between Deleuze and Derrida*, London: Continuum, pp. 183–94.

Rothbaum, Barbara, Larry F. Hodges, David Ready, Ken Graap and Renato D. Alarcon (2001) 'Virtual Reality Exposure Therapy for Vietnam Veterans with Posttraumatic Stress Disorder', *Journal of Clinical Psychology*, 62:8, pp. 617–22.

Ringrose, Jessica, Marnina Gonick, Emma Renold and Lisa Weems (2009) 'Rethinking Agency and Resistance: What Comes after Girl Power?', *Girlhood Studies*, 2:2, pp. 1–9.

Shahrbanian, Shahnaz, Xiaoli Ma, Nicol Korner-Bitensky and Maureen J. Simmonds (2009) 'Scientific Evidence for the Effectiveness of Virtual Reality for Pain Reduction in Adults with Acute or Chronic Pain', in Brenda K. Wiederhold and Giuseppe Riva (eds), *Annual Review of Cybertherapy and Telemedicine*, Amsterdam: IOS Press, pp. 40–3.

Slater, Mel, Bernhard Spanlang, Maria V. Sanchez-Vives and Olaf Blanke (2010) 'First Person Experience of Body Transfer in Virtual Reality', *PLoS ONE*, 5:5, e10564, available at < http://journals.plos.org/plosone/article?id=10.1371/journal.pone.0010564 > (accessed 20 July 2018).

Stark, Hannah (2012) 'Deleuze and Love', *Angelaki*, 17:1, pp. 99–113.

Stark, Hannah and Timothy Laurie (2017) 'Love's Lessons', *Angelaki*, 22:4, pp. 69–79.

Taylor, Paul and Jan Harris (2008) *Critical Theories of Mass Media: Then and Now*, New York: Open University Press.

Valenti, Jessica (2007) *Full Frontal Feminism*, Emeryville, CA: Seal Press.

Wajcman, Judy (2004) *Technofeminism*, Cambridge: Polity Press.

Notes on Contributors

Cheri Lynne Carr is an Associate Professor of Philosophy at LaGuardia Community College, CUNY. A graduate of the University of Memphis, Dr Carr's research is primarily in Ethics, Feminism, Philosophy for Children, and Post-Structuralism. Her recently published book, *Deleuze's Kantian Ethos: Critique as a Way of Life*, explores the potential for a new form of ethical life based on the ideal of critique as the self-perpetuating evaluation of values (Edinburgh University Press, 2018).

Belén Ciancio is a researcher at the National Scientific and Technical Research Council (CONICET), Argentina and has a PhD degree from the Autonomous University of Madrid. Her work is produced in-between cinema and philosophy, feminism and gender. Her most recent publication is 'Estudios de Cine. (Pos) memoria, cuerpo, género' (forthcoming).

Chantelle Gray (PhD) is a Senior Researcher at the Institute for Gender Studies, UNISA (University of South Africa). She is co-convener of the biennial South African Deleuze and Guattari Studies Conference and co-editor of the forthcoming book, *Deleuze and Anarchism*. Chantelle is interested in social justice and political participation/capacitation. She is a member of the editorial collective of *Gender Questions* and served as Editor-in-Chief during 2017.

Francisco Marguch is a graduate student in the Department of Spanish and Portuguese at New York University. He obtained his Licenciatura at the Universidad Nacional de Córdoba, Argentina in 2011 and entered the PhD programme at New York University in the autumn of 2013. His scholarly research focuses on contemporary Southern Cone and Brazilian literatures, queer theory, sexuality studies, contemporary political theory, biopolitics and psychoanalysis.

Bethany Morris is an Assistant Professor of Psychology at Lindsey Wilson College in Kentucky. Her work focuses on critical approaches to psychoanalysis, postmodern philosophy and discourse analysis.

Deleuze and Guattari Studies 12.4 (2018): 612–613
DOI: 10.3366/dlgs.2018.0336
© Edinburgh University Press
www.euppublishing.com/dlgs

S. L. Revoy is a doctoral candidate in the Cultural Studies Program at Queen's University in Kingston, Canada. Their current research interrogates the philosophy, politics and ethics of software design and cybernetic theory, especially focusing on the ways in which these domains affect the development of surveillant technologies and the production of subjectivity.

Ritu Sen Chaudhuri (PhD) is an Associate Professor of Sociology at the West Bengal State University. She has published essays on various issues including feminist theories, women's writing, women's movement, Tagorian novels, and interfaces of sociology, literature and film.

Janae Sholtz is an Associate Professor of Philosophy and the Coordinator of Women's and Gender Studies at Alvernia University. Author of *The Invention of a People: Heidegger and Deleuze on Art and the Political* (Edinburgh University Press, 2015) and co-editor of the forthcoming book, *Deleuze and the Schizoanalysis of Feminism* (Bloomsbury), her research focuses on Continental philosophy, contemporary aesthetics, social and political philosophy, and feminist theory.

Aline Wiame is Assistant Professor of Arts and Philosophy at University Toulouse – Jean Jaurès. Her main research areas are contemporary French philosophy; interactions between philosophy and performance arts; the cartographical reason; and aesthetic consequences of the Anthropocene. She is the author of *Scènes de la défiguration. Quatre propositions entre théâtre et philosophie* (Les Presses du réel, 2016) and she co-edited, with Leonard Lawlor, issue 10.1 of *Deleuze Studies*, 'Deleuze, Ethics and Dramatization' (2016).